THE TO
AND
AROUND

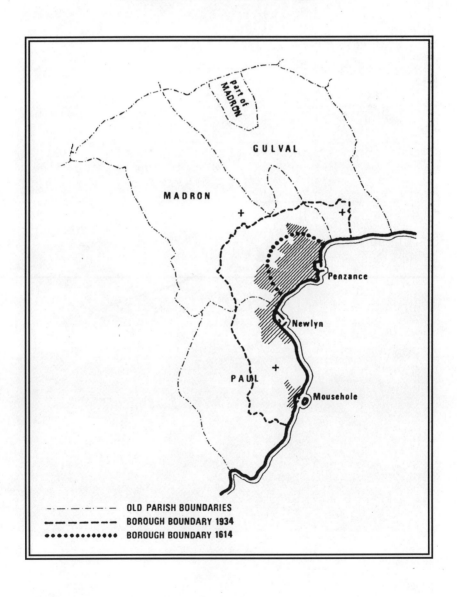

- – – – – – OLD PARISH BOUNDARIES
- – – – – – BOROUGH BOUNDARY 1934
- • • • • • • • • • • • BOROUGH BOUNDARY 1614

Part of MADRON

GULVAL

MADRON

Penzance

Newlyn

PAUL

Mousehole

Dean & Munday, 12.

VIEW of PENZANCE,

With the Su

Sketched, Published, & Sold by Tonkin

the WHERRY MINE,

ing Scenery.

d by Rodda Chapel Street, Penzance.

Preface

This small book is written to mark the time.

It is presented as a gift from Penzance Town Council to our young people, as well as a fund of information for the visitor. You will not find it to be 'heavy history' because resources are already there for the history student or the researcher who has the time and interest for the long study of original documents. But directions are here for a 'reading trail' to follow further.

There are two reasons for my mental sub-title of 'sources and resources'. Firstly, the sources of cultural information about this beautiful area in the far south west of Britain are so many and so varied: formal histories, archaeology texts, linguistic studies, together with photographic, architectural and artistic explorations in book form, legends, plays, films, music and media of all sorts. These sources present anew to us our culture and heritage and leave us a 'spirit'. They are left to us as a legacy from the past people of the place. They offer rich pickings, colourful characters, unique achievements, and much to stimulate our creativity.

Secondly, our inheritance is our resource. We dig in the past to find the evidence and reasons for present situations, to recognise both strengths and weaknesses. Often in the past, the answer to poverty in farming, mining and fishing, was for the native to go abroad and make his or her life elsewhere. This is mirrored in the present by the exodus of young people to find higher education and employment. Emigration may well be the solution for any individual at a particular time, but is no solution for a town or a district. The gain to Cornwall, however, is lots of 'cousin Jacks and Jennies' and a world of Cornish connections. We have within our past the resource for our future.

A refreshed spirit is shining through. There is deeper pride in protecting the beauty of the countryside and coastline. Greater efforts are being made to ensure that old customs flourish. We are looking more closely at improving the quality of our lives through active participation in environmental, cultural, political and educational advances for the area. Some regard this as a return to the glorious past, others to a dynamic future. It should be both.

In preparing this 'plain history of Penzance' I have relied heavily on standard works about the town, and especially on the work of the late Peter Pool which describes Penzance in detail up to 1974. For a view of the wider context of the area and the county as a whole, a good read is Penzance-educated Ian Soulsby's account, *A History of Cornwall*. Nick Sharp of Penlee Museum helped with the selection of photographs employed. Also, I must thank the Cornish cultural historians, Andrew Symons, Alan Kent, Margaret Perry, Charles Thomas, David Giddings, Douglas Williams, Iris Green, Christine North, and members of the Penwith Local History Group, for their reliable and conscientious help to a late-arriving 'compatriot' in the land of Cornwall. To my husband, Philip Budden, I give loving thanks, not only for his careful proofreading of this book, but for bringing me finally to the 'delectable Duchy' (Quiller-Couch's description of Cornwall). In Carew's terms like so many others in the history of this county, I have been 'made Cornish' rather than born so. But, that's a 'proper job' for we!

Melissa Hardie

Contents

CHAPTER 1

CREATING THE PLACE OF PENZANCE

Here at the Land's End there are many parallel stories to be told -- one made up of ancient stones, dug up pots, coins, bracelets and scientific theories, one which is a delicious mixture of geography, legend and romance, and even one in which the living characters are ourselves. To make a single story of these strands, or rather to show where they touch and weave together, is the purpose of this book. Another purpose in the author's mind is to tell this story in such a way that the readers will recognise themselves: "Look! It's us! Warts, wrinkles and all..."

The person native to West Cornwall grows up in an environment where puzzling leftovers of other people's lives, their labours and their customs, are all around. Stones standing upright in the fields, granite boulders lying higgledy-piggledy on the moors, strange constructions of fougous, stone circles and quoits, even a holed stone to crawl through to cure your ills. Here is a former hill fort, there a village of the Iron Age period, and, in Penzance town a tall stone cross of the turn of the last millennium.

Small, walled fields where farmers still work are said to have remained much the same in shape since Iron Age times, and intricate stone walls and narrow lanes seem to have been here forever. Derelict mine chimneys stand dramatically profiled against the skyline. And almost like a miracle, but most decidedly real, sits a castle on a huge boss of granite across a shining sea, reappearing daily in a different light. These are everyday features, often not visited or noticed as unusual by the native born. It may only be when he and she travels away to a different terrain that its unique and beautiful aspects will be recalled and highly valued.

The person who visits Penwith, the most westerly division of Cornwall, is struck immediately by curious words with equally curious pronunciations. Names of places and names of people -- whether saints of old or people of today -- seem to be in a different language, or at least something from an unfamiliar past. And, within the last decade, a translation of place names into Cornish, has begun to be included on road signs and welcome notices for visitors, giving a slight flavour of a special 'land'.

Perhaps the most distinctive and important fact about Cornwall as a whole, and Penwith in particular, is its position geographically. Almost an island, the 326 mile-long coastline outlining the peninsula, has determined its history in several ways. There are no human neighbours nearby except some few at one end not cut off by the Tamar, which line of river divides Cornwall from Devon and the rest of Britain.

The distance from main centres of population and commercial trade on land has meant isolation, on the one hand, from mainstream life in Britain for most of its history. On the other, a unique character was created and a different 'shopfront', a market for trade and communal influence opening onto the world by sea. This has meant both advantages and disadvantages for the settlement and community life of the area, and without doubt a different and perhaps deeper quality of local sentiment and loyalty.

Another feature of Cornish life, which all immigrants and visitors come to learn, is that in a sense, there is one big family living here, and not always, as in all families, an harmonious one. Perhaps a product of its relative isolation in the past, Cornwall is a large, extended family with its aunts and uncles, brothers and cousins, 'reckoned in their dozens'. Most native Cornish families sometime in their histories have inter-married and are

considered relations, even if not on speaking terms. In this literal sense they are well-connected, both at home and abroad. Strangers beware of loose gossip! Memories are long, and the Celtic memory even longer.

What is true for Cornwall, is even more certain for the area which a late friend, Gerald Priestland, called 'Cornwall's Cornwall' or 'west of Hayle River', the title he gave to his delightful biography of his adopted land. He suggests that Penwith itself might become an island if the sea rose about 50 feet; 'Spiritually, it is one already'.

One can only add, that if Penwith were an island, there is no doubt that being the district seat of government and with a larger commercial base, harbourside and shopping centre, Penzance would be its capital (people in St. Ives just might argue the toss). In the past this was not always so. There is much to learn about and from the land upon which we now live, before Penzance was a place. Let us look back in order to work forward to the present time.

The last ice age and its results for Cornwall
When first a visitor to Cornwall I was often struck by the similarity of Cornwall to Brittany, their music, and their place-names. I knew little about their shared Celtic background, or of the long-time association of the peoples of the southern British coast and of 'little Britain' in France. The presence of St. Michael's Mount in Cornwall and its giant neighbour Mont St. Michel off the coast of Normandy was equally intriguing. Is the water between us just our way of passing the salt? I needed to know more.

Before the last ice age was complete, the territory that included the present-day peninsula of Cornwall as well as Brittany, was one vast polar desert where no one lived as far as is known. The rising of the seas, as the ice melted at a rate of some 1.15mm average per year, meant that the land bridge between the continent and the now island of Britain was gradually submerged under water.

As the temperature rose, vegetation and trees could begin their lives but as the melting continued some of these also disappeared under the water. Cornwall's southern coast was shaped by the submergence of a low plain upon which forests had grown. One of the submerged forests lies in Mounts Bay. And, there are stories which place much more -- that magical land of Lyonnesse -- between the mainland and the Isles of Scilly, phenomena also arising from a submerged landscape though at a much later date (in the first millennium AD). These physical characteristics of the Land's End area give rise to many anecdotes and legends that have been told and re-told in the oral traditions of the native people. Equally they give fertile ground for geological and archaeological exploration. So, already in the telling of our 'creation myth' we have the elements for a rich mix of imagination and science.

The early in-comers to the Land's End
The first comers (Mesolithic) to the peninsula are thought to have been roving groups of people (tribes) who hunted for wild animals, gathered berries and other vegetation, and also made use of what they could harvest from the sea. The evidence of their lives comes to us in finding flint tools for opening of shellfish, for the treatment of animal hides, and for making weapons for hunting. These people are called in pre-history terms the 'hunter/gatherers'.

Permanent settlements have been found in the Land's End area from about 4000 BC, as tribal generations moved into the Neolithic period. Gradually small groups of people were moving westward in these times, bringing with them knowledge of farming, the construction of huts and houses, and the making of pottery.

An early settlement of great importance was at nearby Carn Brea (at Camborne-Redruth), the examination of which revealed an enclosure constructed on a hilltop, similar in pattern to others in north-west Europe at the same time. The current small castle sitting on Carn Brea is of much later construction (19th C.). This was the period, over a 2000 year span, that most of the monuments were erected and constructed, like standing stones (menhirs), chamber tombs and other stone configurations called quoits, dolmens and cromlechs. Such feats of strength and industry show that people had begun to organise themselves to work together for recognised family and community purposes, though today we are not sure of the meaning and use of their constructions.

The next group of settlers to arrive and join the 'melting pot' are called the Beaker people, identified as a separate grouping because of their special style of pottery, reddish-brown and decorated and the distinctive manner of their burial routines. They arrived in Cornwall from about 2500 BC, and this may have been by sea from the Iberian peninsula via Wales and Ireland. The beauty of their designs seems to remind us of the Mediterranean. With them comes the term the Bronze Age, because they knew about mineral working in copper and tin to make the alloy bronze, from which they crafted more advanced implements -- tools, pots, and weaponry.

The Men-an-Tol, near Madron

Monument building continued, some of it possibly territorial marking, others for ceremonial -- burial and worship -- and storage purposes. it is fairly certain that stone circles like the Merry Maidens in Penwith, are a product of these times. It is also clear from archaeological finds that in Bronze Age in Cornwall, aside from farming, animal husbandry, and fighting (!), that trading had begun with other lands such as Wales, Ireland and Brittany and perhaps even further afield.

Come the Celts

Knowledge of iron-working spread from Europe throughout Britain by the beginning of the 1st millennium BC, and coming with these developments in Cornwall were Celtic tribal people. The gradual immigration of Celtic settlers over the eight centuries prior to the Christian era have left indelible marks upon the Cornish, meshing together with the then residents their language, customs and skills. It is important to try to learn and understand what we can about them in more detail, because of the claim of the Cornish to be a 'Celtic' nation: one of the six Celtic nationalities of Welsh, Cornish and Breton (called Brythonic or British Celts) and the Irish, Scots and Manx (called Goidelic Celts).

Exactly who the Celts were, where they came from, what their history, religious practices and characters were, are matters of great interest and debate. We have learned about them from legend and from written reports of other places they invaded and settled, and also from records of how they were in their turn driven out, or beaten in wars at different times. We are told that they were tribal people, coming from the lower Danube region of middle Europe and that they spread throughout mainland Europe, specifically Gaul, and to all corners of the British Isles. Much later, when thoroughly mingled genetically, they would, of course, spread out across the world through emigration, war, and even tourism. For a short time in the 4th C. BC, Rome itself was dominated by the Celts but managed to push them out again, and in the 3rd C. BC tribes called *keltoi* warred against Greece.

Lanyon Quoit

Written records report the existence of druids or early philosopher-scientists amongst the Celts. Tribal legends demonstrated essentially democratic characteristics (government by assembly), and high respect and regard for women. They were also seen as warlike, fierce in battle, and even bloodthirsty, the women fighting alongside the men. [Boudicca (Boadicea) was a Celt.] Religiously, they were known to honour the human head as the principal part of a person, and to decapitate and retain heads as symbolic of obtaining the spirit and essence of the beheaded. Their beliefs included the existence of a spirit world parallel to the land of the living. They are also known to have created the oldest document in a Celtic language in the form of a sophisticated calendar dating from the 1st C. of the Christian era.

The greatest remains in Penwith from this Celtic period -- called the Iron Age -- are at Castle-an-Dinas and Chysauster Village, both within a mile of each other inland from Gulval and east of Newmill, and at Chun Castle, inland from Morvah. Castle-an-Dinas was a defended hill-fort with views in all directions. Chysauster with its storerooms, houses, and system of fields marked out nearby (many of which are now destroyed) was a farming settlement, now open to the public by English Heritage. A similar field system for farming can still be viewed near Zennor on the north coast, preserved by the National Trust. Chun, Ch'un, Chyoon, or Chywoon (different spellings for the same place) is perhaps the most remarkable of all the Cornish hill-castles. Its ramparts were known to be all of 15 feet high until the 1840s, when stone was taken to build the north pier in Penzance.

The Romans in Britain & the Christian Era
By the time of the Roman invasion of Britain, Cornwall's livelihood was already being made with a pattern of activities for which it is still traditionally known: fishing, farming, tin streaming and metal-working as well as pottery making. The trade in tin was well established, especially with the Mediterranean area and the general access to Cornwall was almost solely by sea.

One legend which pops up occasionally (amusingly resurrected by Gerald Priestland in a BBC radio broadcast entitled 'Did Jesus visit Ding Dong?') concerns the boy Jesus and the tin trade. The legend reports that Jesus accompanied his uncle, Joseph of Arimathea, on a sea voyage to Cornwall, to help collect a shipment of tin for the Phoenicians. Priestland spent an hour or more on his Sunday radio slot asking locals around his Cornish home near Ding Dong Mine in Madron parish, what they thought about this story? The consensus was that no one was aware of this rumour, and one wag offered the comment: "I don't rightly remember he was here or no!"

I thought to myself as I listened "This is just how new legends begin and

gossip tries to re-write history." I have since learned that at least three other places in Cornwall make the same claim, and Glastonbury, Somerset as well.

The First Millennium AD
The first exploration of Britain by Julius Caesar was in 55 BC, but it was a short visit and did not include Cornwall. Information, however, was available to him of its existence. Before his second and full invasion, Diodorus Siculus wrote in 30 BC, that the people living around Land's End (called Belerion) were friendly to strangers and were civilised because of contact with traders. He also described how they prepared the tin for trading exchange. It is believed that Siculus gathered this information based on a 4th C. BC sailing voyage made by Pytheas of Marseilles, so it seems that those of the Land's End had been 'civilised' for quite a long time. After the full-scale invasion by the Romans in AD 43, it was more than ten years before the legions arrived in the south-west and established their fortification at Isca Dumnoniorum (Exeter). For the most part the invaders left the areas and peoples beyond Exeter to their own devices. The laws of Rome made occasional forays into the far west, but generally it was too far for too little gain.

Taxes were collected, and finds of Roman coins indicate that trade for tin through about three centuries commenced soon, declined, and then picked up again between the Romans and the Cornish. Life progressed much the same in Land's End with farming, fishing, tin streaming and working being the main occupations. Scattered communities, the continued use of round houses and enclosures, and the normal trading patterns by sea remained.

In the Roman governmental pattern, the lands of West Somerset, Devon and Cornwall were known as Civitas Dumnoniorum, the centre for which was Exeter, and the people of these areas were Dumnonii, the name used by classical writers to describe the tribal groups living here. Though people certainly lived in the far west of Dumnonia in and around the Land's End, these settlements remained scattered and seemingly tribal in nature, perhaps with local leaders or chieftains who might have had some responsibility to authorities at Exeter. But in the daily round of life at Land's End, the Romans made no difference.

Before the Romans finally withdrew their military protection and administration from Britain in AD 410, other settlers had begun to move in from Germanic lands (Saxons) to the east coast of Britain, and from Ireland to western parts of Scotland and Wales. Some of these people too would become newcomers to Cornish lands (not clearly defined) and join people who were becoming known as Cornovii, a section of the Dumnonii. Equally, it appears that Dumnonii, Cornovii and people from West Wales were emigrating and colonising Armorica (the ancient name for Brittany) and Galicia on the northern coast of Spain, creating Celtic-speaking settlements on the mainland of Europe. Most of this history we learn from the study of language and the finding of characteristic words (called 'loan words' by scholars) in different geographical areas as commonly used by their people.

The Men Scryfa, the writing or written stone

There are words found written on some standing stones, one of note in the Penwith area being the *Men Scryfa*, the writing stone, and these writings form historical documents that aid us in understanding the early history of Cornwall. The writing found on these stones is a mixture, a few in the Irish script called Ogham, others in a mixture of Ogham and Latin, and some in Latin only. By reading the script, we learn names of tribal chieftains, perhaps local 'kings' which are also sometimes found in legends, then by taking the two together -- archaeological finds and results of oral histories -- we begin to piece together possible 'pictures of the past'.

The Land of Saints
As everyone knows, Cornwall has been described as the 'land of Saints', and many saints' names are commemorated in parishes, villages and towns all over the county. What these names tell us is more where Christian influences arrived from and more-or-less when, rather than much about who they were individually, or even if they came in person. Because of cross-settlement, similar saintly people, sometimes the same by name and sometimes not, are remembered in Ireland, Wales, Scotland, and Brittany.

Since it is probable that West Cornwall's people hardly noticed the coming and going of the Romans who finally withdrew from Britain in the 5th C., it may have been more than a hundred years before they realised the significance of the Saxon arrival in British lands. Protected by their isolated geography and by militants who fought the invaders further east, they were left to develop their own Celtic culture and traditions in their own ways.

Though there was some familiarity with Christianity through trading partners, immigrants and travellers before AD 500, there was an increased flow of Christian influences after. Some of these would have been escapees seeking refuge from Saxon invasions elsewhere, but primarily they came from Wales and Ireland. These were the peoples who shared Celtic origins and language and like Cornwall, had avoided the strong changes which life under the Romans had introduced to central England.

Most of the saints we know more by legend than by fact, and often the information is confusing because it is well mixed with poetic licence and story-telling. For example, St. Ia was supposed to have floated into St. Ives on a leaf from Ireland (was she in a boat of bark with some leaves left on?). And the famous St. Piran whose flag has been adopted for Cornwall 'arrived on a millstone' also from Ireland. There is probably a truth embedded in this seemingly strange story but we do not know what it is!

But their purposes were clear: establishing chapels for contemplation, prayer and the hermit life, while also creating monastic dwellings for teaching and converting the pagans. These 'saints' were missionaries, both men and women, for Christianity rather than canonised saints in the more modern sense. Whereas one Christian 'Brother' or 'Sister' might settle and live out a life here, encouraging others to join in, another would come, establish a settlement of some kind and then proceed on to Brittany to do the same. In return, it is clear that some of the saints' names that we remember in Cornwall are taken from the Breton immigrations in the reverse direction.

The missionaries arrived with broader knowledge and the ability to write, to make records, and to use symbols confirming their presence, such as the use of the Chi/Rho sign on a burial stone. The Christianity that emerged from the meshing of customs, traditions, and enthusiasms of the pagans with the new Christian influences was distinctive, and created Celtic saints on home ground in Cornwall and in all Celtic areas. The special blend of Christianity and Celticism that resulted remained a part of the Roman Catholic Church, but also differed in the development of its own traditions. There was always a suspicion on the part of the Roman ecclesiastics that Celtic churchmen mixed some of their pre-Christian ways into their Catholicism. Important areas of contention were the dating of religious festivals, especially the Easter cycle of events (Holy Week) and matters of priestly dress.

The Holy Wells
A good example of the adoption process by which Christianity took over

the Celtic cultural spirit in Cornwall is found in the study of so-called 'holy wells'. Whereas the Celts worshipped natural springs because pure water was necessary to life and was itself 'alive', the missionary seeking a place to settle would also want a place for baptising. Wells were obvious and central places for social life and festivity, to be celebrated and decorated with offerings. From Celtic times they were also assumed to have curative powers, and the sick would be passed through the waters with special rituals and at special times, especially in early May to renew their strength in the spring (called Beltane) of the year.

The most famous in the Penzance area are the Madron Well and the St. Levan Well, each with an accompanying baptistry, the Sancreed Holy Well and the nearby Chapel Euny Well, now ruined. Lesser known are those at Trewoofe (near Lamorna) which cured gout, and the Alsia (pronounced 'Ailyer') Well, which was helpful with toothache. There are others at Zennor, Morvah, Newmill, and even a 'lost one' at Gulval (St. Gudwal) and throughout the whole of Cornwall.

Saints of the Land's End
The saints who have left their names in the Land's End area and all over Cornwall are many, some 170 in all when immigrants are added to those they attracted to the Christian life. Because of the treacherous sea passage of the Land's End, most traffic from the Mediterranean and continent used routes through Cornwall. One of these was the Camel-Fowey passage used by many missionaries coming from South Wales. The other was the Hayle-Marazion route.

The whole of western Britain was served through these 'routeways' from earliest times until the end of the Dark Ages. The traffic was substantial and, of course, international, bringing a cosmopolitan flavour to Penwith, which consequently was much less an isolated backwater than one might suspect. Apparently there were defensive forts or sites along these routes where local chieftains guarded against intrusion.

Breaca was one of three missionaries (the others being Crowan and Germoe) arriving at the Hayle Estuary from Ireland and managed to escape the notice of ruler Tewdrig, who routinely enjoyed executing missionaries (for example, he killed Gwinear, a 6th C. Irish saint, commemorated at Gwinear near Hayle). Breaca established her work at Breage between Penzance and Helston.

Buryan (Berriona, Beriana, Beryan) came from Ireland where she was the daughter of a Munster chieftain, in the 6th C. and established her foundation four miles east of Land's End at St. Buryan. Her feast day is 1 May, usually associated with the pre-Christian (Celtic) goddess of fertility.

Erc, (St. Erth) was an Irish missionary, said to be the brother of St. Ia (St. Ives) and St. Euny.

Gulval (Latin: Wolvela) seemingly refers to a female saint who may have had her dwelling at Bosulval, near Newmill village (tr. 'dwelling place of Wolvela') in the 6th or 7th C.

Just (Justin, Yestin) was a son of St. Gerent as was St. Selevan (whose son was St. Cuby), and is remembered both in Penwith and on the Roseland peninsula.

Ludgvan   Ludgvan Feast celebrates St. Ludewon, but little is known of this name. Local Cornish folk call this village 'Lidgen'.

Madron (St. Madernus), is the site of the Madron Well and baptistery, but it is not known whether this saint was Welsh or Irish. The feast day is 17 May.

Paul Aurelian (St. Pol de Leon) was a 6th C Welsh missionary who took 12 followers and emigrated to Brittany via Cornwall, where his sister, St. Sitofolla, was living at Mount's Bay with others. He found another location for them at Gwavas Lake, lying between the villages of Newlyn and Mousehole. And he left his own name on the nearby village of Paul where the church there is dedicated to him. Later he went on to Brittany and was consecrated the Bishop of Leon.

Sancreed (St. Sancreed) was said to have accidentally killed his father and went to work as a hermit/swineherd in penitence. From this disaster he started a ministry.

Selevan is said to be the brother of Just, son of St. Erbyn, and is remembered at the church at St. Levan, where there is a holy well and the ruins of his original chapel.

Senara is a female saint about which nothing is known, remembered in the name of nearby Zennor.

Finally, of course, what the missionaries established and the Saxon invasion nurtured, though accidentally, was a strong Catholic Cornwall. These were hard and uncertain times, and through the centuries in which the Saxons and the Angles fought to gain their hold upon Britain, we know little through lack of records. What we do know, however, is that due to being in such a peripheral location geographically, West Cornwall in particular was left to itself and to its general subsistence level of poverty. The farming, fishing and mining folk were often the last to know, and therefore the last to change in custom or language. For these reasons, the Celtic culture remained strongest here, and the Cornish language continued longest to be spoken.

These are called the Dark Ages, because they were characterised by violent and destructive tribal warfare and we cannot see into them due to lack of literature and written records. But, it appears that what may not have been written down, whether it was through illiteracy or suppression, we have remaining in oral tradition and legend. From these same times of conflict and conversion come the stories of King Arthur fighting against the Saxons in a variety of Celtic countries in addition to Cornwall, and King Mark, Tristan and other semi-historical figures which still live today in novels and poetry, films and drama, music and song.

St. Michael's Mount

No person visiting Penzance, Newlyn or Mousehole or living at the Land's End can ignore the wondrous presence in the bay of the Mount itself. Its closest land base is to the ancient market town of Marazion. That interesting name translates from Cornish to English as 'Market Jew', which is also the name of the main shopping street of Penzance, which leads out of town toward Marazion, in the same way that many towns all over Britain have a 'London Road'.

Into medieval times there were two separate places on the land across from the Mount, called marghas yow (Thursday market) and marghas byghan (little market), and the combination of these two became

Marazion, nothing to do with the Jews. At low tide the Mount is connected to Marazion by a stone causeway a half-mile in length. Its origins as a trading post (probably the one called Ictis in ancient writings) before the Christian era, later a religious house and shrine for pilgrims, and also as a military defence installation are documented in its long history. Buildings, domestic and religious, have come and gone, but what exists there now dates from the 14th C. on, with additions, repairs and re-building as necessary and possible.

By the time of the Domesday Survey (1086), the Norman conquerors recorded that the Mount had already been given, by Edward the Confessor twenty years before, as a token for the 'salvation of my soul and the souls of my parents' for the use of the Benedictine order. But, with the invading Normans in 1068, when William's conquest of the West Country was complete, it was part of a parcel of gifts given to Robert, Count of Mortain, for his support.

Keeping the most profitable of more than 250 West Country manors for himself he gave the Mount to the monks of Mont St. Michel, in his home country of Normandy. Amongst other gifts he granted to them the privilege of a Thursday market. Though virtually nothing is known about the life of the monks there in the 11th C., their job was fairly straightforward: to farm the attached land, feed those living there, sell the surplus, and forward this income together with donations from pilgrims back to the mother-house in Normandy.

Penzance, its name and its origins
Penzance itself is not associated with any particular saint, nor do we know when it came into being as a place with this name. The name translates from Cornish as Pen sans (holy headland) and refers to a headland of granite that extends from the hills into Mount's Bay forming a bay within the larger bay. The modern use of this smaller sheltered bay has become the open-air swimming pool. Originally, however, there was sited there a small chapel supposedly dedicated by the local fishing folk to St. Anthony

(of Padua), regarded as their patron saint.

It seems that soon after the chapel was constructed, it was incorporated into a fish cellar near the pier, of which fragments only remained by 1800. A fragment of a granite cross, from the early 12th C., was removed to St. Mary's Churchyard (now the Parish Church) in 1850, where it still can be seen. Its features are now somewhat indistinct and damaged but pictures Christ in loincloth and a seated Madonna holding a child.

None of the settlements around the Mount's Bay -- Mousehole, Newlyn, Penzance, or Marazion -- is mentioned in the Domesday Survey of 1086. The first notice of Penzance found to date is in 1284 when it is mentioned in the Assize Rolls. "For the whole of this period (to 1500), it remained uncertain whether Penzance, Mousehole or Marazion would emerge as the chief port and trading centre of Mount's Bay, and the other towns often seemed in important respects to be substantially ahead of Penzance". (P. Pool)

Less than 20,000 people lived in the whole of Cornwall at the time of the Norman Conquest. How many of these were living in the general area of Penzance is not known, but even by the 1660s, the number was unlikely to have been as many as a thousand, little more than an overgrown village. Nonetheless, the establishment of towns and the expansion of mining activities by the time the Duchy of Cornwall was created in 1337, had brought more than three times that many into the county, and would continue to do so in waves and in different areas as mining methods changed.

The Manor of Alwareton, in which Penzance and its district sat, as an unnamed part, was owned by an alien Saxon lord named Alward. At the Conquest, like St. Michael's Mount, Alwareton (now Alverton on the west side of Market Jew Street) was also granted to Robert de Mortain and continued in ownership of the Earls of Cornwall until about 1230 when it was given to the Tyes family. Almost a hundred years later the head of the family, Henry, Lord Tyes participated in a revolt against the King, was tried and executed. At that point his lands were taken away by the crown, but restored to his sister, Alice de Lisle, some ten years later. Her husband had also been executed at the time of the revolt, so she was left to resurrect what she could to support her family. Here in 1332, we meet an original and enterprising woman who played a very important role in the development of the town. To her was granted the rights to organise and maintain the markets and fairs of Penzance, and this was the strategically important sign of a community that worked and played together. In the same year she was also granted the income from a new fair in Mousehole, a village which had already benefited from markets and fairs for some 40 years before.

From the religious or ecclesiastical position, Penzance was located within the boundaries of the Parish of Madron. To the west, where both Newlyn and Mousehole stand was the land of the Parish of Paul. The Parish of Gulval abutted it to the east. One of the possessions of Lord Tyes , at the time of his execution, was a Chapel of St. Mary within the boundaries of Alwareton. This became licensed as a chapel of ease (i.e., closer to the parishioners of Penzance) to Madron Parish in 1379, where the Catholic services were regularly held. There was also a Chapel called St. Clare (also spelled Cleer, and Clere), which though it is no longer there, is remembered in the name of the street of the same name, where the district offices, the swimming baths, Penwith College and the cricket grounds now cluster.

Two Cornish Uprisings
These small villages around the Mount's Bay were not, of course, completely isolated from larger, political upheavals of their day. Ian Soulsby provides two quotes of interest concerning the character of the Cornish as the pushing and shoving began between rival kings of England and Scotland, together with the taxation exacted to support those struggles. And, soon, the continuing religious strife between Catholics and the Protestants was to peak in the Reformation.

"...the folk of these parts are quite extraordinary, being of a rebellious temper, and obdurate in the face of attempts to teach and correct" (Adam de Carlton, Archdeacon of Cornwall, 1342)
'The tinners had a particularly notorious reputation; a century and a half (1497) later they could still be regarded as "twelve thousand of the roughest and most mutinous men in England".'

By adding the temperament to the time, we find a lethal mix that was to explode in several directions. When the Royal Commissioners were appointed to assess tax in Cornwall, it was clear that this money was wanted to support Henry VII's campaign against the forces of James IV of Scotland. This, then, was the English attacking our Celtic kin in Scotland, and the Cornish would not have that!

Michael Joseph Angof (Cornish for 'The Smith'), a blacksmith from St. Keverne on the Lizard, led an uprising of angry Cornishmen, protesting against the taxes. Together with men from Madron and other west Cornwall families, and collecting supporters all the way through Cornwall amongst the working men of the farms and mines as well all sections of the Cornish communities, the march gathered force as it moved over the Tamar and on to London. There 15,000 militants met up with up to 25,000 for the Crown at Blackheath. The outcome was disastrous for the Cornish ringleaders and their troops of ill-provisioned men with few weapons. An Gof and Thomas Flamanck and the dissident Lord Audley, the primary leaders, were executed, the first two hung, drawn and quartered, and the latter beheaded. Many of the followers were killed but the vanquished majority slipped away walking their long trek back to their homes in the west.

That same year (1497) an imposter and pretender to the throne of England, Perkin Warbeck, landed on the Land's End shore near Sennen with approximately 200 followers. Having garnered Scots' support and been married to Lady Katherine Gordon in Edinburgh, he could see how he could use the Cornish fury to his advantage. He hot-footed it from

Scotland through Ireland to Cornwall with his entourage.

At Bodmin Warbeck declared himself Richard IV, to supporters numbering some 3,000 and marched on to Exeter. By the time he had arrived at the gates of Exeter backed by some 6,000 supporters, the military leader Daubeny and army turned up again (as at Blackheath) with a force to rout the second Cornish uprising against the Crown. Warbeck deserted but was captured and executed in due course. The defeated Cornish, angry at being fooled, were further humiliated by being heavily fined by the King for their participation in yet another dangerous and disloyal confrontation. War reparations, after all, were not much different than taxes, as far as Henry was concerned.

In legend and literature
The Land's End of post-Roman and medieval Cornwall is fascinating culturally, and many legends, stories and tales about it have been collected.

Lyonnesse
One of the most famous is the story of Lyonnesse. A fertile region once united the Scilly Islands with western Cornwall. A people called the Silures inhabited this tract of land, and they were remarkable for their hard work and piety. No less than 140 churches stood in that region, which is now submerged by the sea, and the rocks called the Seven Stones -- or in Cornish, Lethowsow -- are said to mark the place of a great city. Exactly how the flood occurred is not explained, though it is said that one of the ancestors of the Trevelyan (of St. Veep) family had time to flee the flooding upon a horse, and made it to the mainland without being drowned. And there are tales of hearing the ringing of the church bells on a calm night.

The Giants
There are many stories about West Cornwall as the land of giants. One story, concerning the giants of St. Michael's Mount, takes place in the Penzance area. In the days of the giants of Cornwall, the Mount was known as the White Rock in the wood, or in Cornish Carreg luz en kuz. In this

wood, a giant named Cormoran decided that he would build a castle, so that he could keep watch over the neighbouring country. Cormoran began to pile up white granite rock from the neighbouring hill. His wife, Cormelian assisted him in the process by carrying the rocks in her apron.

One day while Cormoran was sleeping, she decided that one stone would do as well as any other and so broke off a piece of greenstone rock, and took it towards the artificial hill, without being seen by her husband. When Cormelian passed by her husband, Cormoran awoke, and when he saw his wife was carrying a green stone instead of a white one, he gave her a great kick. Her apron-string broke and the stone fell on the sand, and there it has since remained. The giantess died and the mass of rock - now known as 'The Chapel Rock' by Marazion - became her monument.

The Last Wolf in Britain

Robert Hunt also records an interesting story concerning the native population of wolves of these islands. According to superstition the last native wolf lived in the forest of Ludgvan near Penzance. The last of his species was apparently a gigantic specimen, and terrible was the havoc he caused in the local flocks of sheep. Tradition tells us that he also carried off a local child. This could not be endured and so all the peasantry turned out and this last famous wolf was captured at Rospeath, the name of a farm still existing in Ludgvan.

Tristan and Iseult

One of the earliest surviving versions of the story of Tristan and Isolde (there are many spellings of her name, and perhaps Iseult is the most accurate, Cornish Eselt, British Adsiltia) almost certainly originated from a Cornish author, or a person who knew intimately the southern coast of Cornwall. St. Michael's Mount and Mount's Bay itself is an incredible panorama, and perhaps all too difficult for any writer to resist. The 12th C. French poet Beroul tells of how Ogrin the hermit of the story 'went to St Michael's Mount because of all the fine goods that can be found there'. A market of this kind certainly forms an important backdrop for much activity around the Penzance area.

Market Jew Street and Marazion

'Market Jew' features in much of the folklore and literature of Cornwall, though there is often confusion as to whether this is referring to the major shopping street in Penzance or one of the older spellings of the nearby market town of Marazion. The earliest Thursday market was established at Marazion, as explained, and the Penzance street came to have the same name because it leads out of town toward Marazion. Later Penzance was to have its own Thursday market.

Market Jew, as a place, however, does feature in the second play of the Cornish Mystery Play trilogy known as *Ordinalia*. In the year 2000, due to an award from the Millennium Festival Fund, the first of these plays is being performed in and by the wider community at the Playing Place in St. Just. Community mystery plays of this type were very popular in Europe during the medieval period. As part of the movement of popular Catholicism to teach Christianity in the language of the people, the writer wove together either biblical narrative or saints' lives onto local landscape and culture. Though it is supposed that *Ordinalia* was written at the Glasney College, Penryn, perhaps by one of the brethren there, the playwright has woven in a piece of west Cornwall in the following sequence where the torturers are looking for a blacksmith to make the nails for Christ's cross:

> Ho there, good fellow, ho!
> Tell me forthwith,
> if you know where there are nails
> to fix Him to the cross:
> Go and ask, without delay,
> of the smith in Market Jew.

The reading trail for Chapter 1

William Bottrell (Editor, 1873) *Traditions and Hearthside Stories of West Cornwall*, Beare and Sons, Penzance.

P. Berresford Ellis (1974) *The Cornish Language and Its Literature*, Routledge and Kegan Paul, London.

Marjorie Filbee (1996) *Celtic Cornwall*, Constable, London.

Robert Hunt (Editor, 1865), *Popular Romances of the West of England*, Hotten, London.

O.J. Padel (1988) *A Popular Dictionary of Cornish Place-Names*, Newmill: Alison Hodge.

Peter Pool (1974) *The History of the Town and Borough of Penzance*, Corporation of Penzance.

Ian Soulsby (1986) *A History of Cornwall*, Phillimore & Co., Sussex.

Charles Thomas (1985) *Exploration of a Drowned Landscape, Archaeology and History of the Isles of Scilly*, B. T. Batsford, London.

(1986) *Celtic Britain*, Thames and Hudson, London.

CHAPTER 2

THE FORMING AND RE-FORMING OF A PLACE 1500-1720

The 16th C. in the Mount's Bay area was to be a momentous one, perhaps the most upsetting one to its ordinary pattern of daily life, and to its speech and language. The two uprisings of Cornishmen in 1497, with tinners being some of the most fierce and fearless, had ended in humiliation and debt. Henry VII had been, on the whole, gracious in his defeat of them; perhaps he recalled the support of these western followers when he took the Crown from Richard III at Bosworth Field.

Except for the execution of the rebel leaders Angof, Flamanck and Audley, and the pretender Warbeck (a Belgian), Henry took few reprisals after those rebellions and let the westerners return to their homes without undue bother. Nevertheless he imposed and collected fines from villages and labouring families all over Cornwall.

The penalised were in areas already poor and distressed in their barely sustainable employment of mining, farming and fishing, and altogether unhappy and rebellious in their servitude to mainly absentee landlords. Some historians say that the heavy fines kept the impoverished Cornish quiet for another 50 years, but others that the resentment incurred through these incidents still has influence and echo today. Certainly, it appears that in the public mind, from this period, the Cornish were seen as a people of lost causes.

Harbour

The manor of Alverton (Alwareton of old) belonged to the Crown, when in 1512, Henry VIII granted to his tenants in Penzance (spelled at this time 'Pensans') the dues and payments that were levied at the harbour to incoming and outgoing sea-traders. He granted this in return for a promise that the locals would keep and repair the quay and defences that would guard both shipping arrangements and the town itself. Here were the critical and, in that sense, important western reaches of the kingdom. They were vulnerable to attack and invasion just as they were open to trade. Sticking out as the peninsula does into the high seas, this is an important point which has had relevance to the 20th C., due to the coastal defences believed necessary to repel invasion in the World Wars I and II.

King Henry's 'gift' can be viewed in modern terms, like the granting of rights to hold markets and fairs, as an early form of local devolution or town organisation. Some group or community of workers had to be present to receive these grants and make them work. However, the profits would accrue to the lucky agents and friends of the King, and these might seldom, if ever, live locally or have much local connection. Nevertheless, the document proving the grant of the harbour dues is the earliest piece of evidence of town formation in the possession of Penzance Town Council today. It would not be until a century later (1614) that Penzance would become a Borough Town by Charter, recognition of importance that neither Newlyn nor Mousehole would independently achieve.

In his detailed *History of Penzance*, Peter Pool summed up the entry point of the Land's End area:

"Thus, at the end of the Middle Ages, in 1500, Penzance, Mousehole, Marazion and St. Ives each had a chapel, a quay, markets and fairs. Marazion had the greatest antiquity, St. Ives the greatest degree of independence from its [ecclesiastic] parish, and no prophet would have had much reason to suppose that Penzance was destined to overtake the others and become the chief town and port of Penwith."

When the King's Librarian, young John Leland, visited Cornwall in his tour of Henry VIII's lands, a little later in 1538, he added more to our knowledge of the immediate area. Frank Halliday in his version of *A History of Cornwall* gives this summary of Leland's report:

"And so to the tin-working region of the far west. Not very long ago, he [Leland] was told, good tall ships used to sail up the Hayle river as far as St. Erth, but now the haven was choked with sand brought down from the tin-works. Sand, though this time blown from beaches, was also the curse of St. Ives, for in the course of the last twenty years most of the houses, and even the little pier, had been 'sore oppressid or overcoverid with Sandes that the stormy Windes and Rages castith up there'... From St. Ives he rode along the north coast to St. Just and the Land's End, then back by St. Buryan, whose dean and prebenderies 'almost be never ther', to Mousehole, 'a praty Fyschar Town'. He noted piers at Newlyn, Penzance and St. Michael's Mount, where were also 'howses with shoppes for fyschermen...From Penwith he returned along the south coast, first calling on Sir William Godolphin, whose tin-works were the greatest in all Cornwall..."

The Reformation in Cornwall
Without re-telling the whole history of the Christian Reformation proper, any genuine understanding of Britain, Cornwall and Penzance today, requires some knowledge of what occurred in the 16th C. The figure of Martin Luther dominated that history in Europe, just as later, in Cornwall, the persons of John and Charles Wesley would dominate the 18th C.

Saxon-born Luther, the son of a miner, and well educated in law and theology at German universities, left the purely academic world to join an Augustinian order of hermit monks at the age of 21. The greatest shock to him was in discovering the immoral life of priests and cardinals of the Roman church. In 1517 he made his famous proclamation on the abuse by priests of their power of forgiving sins (indulgences that were purchased to avoid penance). These open charges were to send shock waves around the Christian world, and it was possible because of a scientific and technical development: the invention of the printing press.

While the invention of the printing press itself may have had no particular influence in Cornwall at that time, what this initial medium allowed was the wide-spread sharing of unrest and disaffection, wherever that would arise. Here began the ultimate breakdown of authorities that had been previously known, especially those of the Church that had grown wealthy and in some ways grossly corrupt. What Luther wanted originally was a return to a kind of simple Christianity, without its systematic control over the individual person. He believed in a person justified by faith alone.

The second major figure in the Reformation period was John Calvin, French educated, and a generation further on from Luther. Much stricter in his insistence upon the authority of the Bible, Calvin carried out most of his ministry and teaching in Geneva, Switzerland in the 1550s. He laid down religious rules that should be strictly adhered to, if members of the church were to be saved. At base was his conviction that religion is a matter of personal conviction and personal conscience.

So, in Europe, the scene was set for revolution. In Britain, Henry VIII had been taxing his peoples heavily for sums to support his wars with the French. When peace came in 1525, he could turn his mind to argue further with the Pope over the refusal of Rome to sanction his divorce from Catherine of Aragon. With Thomas Cromwell at his side, changes were to be made progessively throughout his lands, which would loosen the dominating power of the Roman Catholic Church and its priests and monks.

In 1534, Parliament passed an 'Act of Supremacy' that made the King the supreme Head of the Church of England. Soon after, Acts were passed which dissolved the monasteries and returned their endowments (their money and their assets) to the Crown.

In 1545 the finance provided by the Tyes family as endowment for St. Mary's Chapel (of Ease) at Penzance was taken away by the Crown, despite pleas to the contrary. The argument for supporting St. Mary's was that the Madron Parish Church was too far away to walk for the parishioners, and, if they were away from the village so long, they could not defend themselves against foreign attack because they would not be there to guard their harbour and town. To our ears this sounds far-fetched, but there was substance to it. Since there was little transport, and attendance at church for everyone was more or less compulsory (soon to be made so at risk of imprisonment), the people of the Mount's Bay area did have to be vigilant. Boats could land at any time, through accident or design, and disgorge their crews. A good example of such an unexpected invasion was to come...but 50 years later. But, not until 1680, was the Chapel to be once again endowed in Penzance.

Cornish monasteries were probably no more corrupt than others, but nevertheless they were to be shut down, Glasney College at Penryn included. The Benedictine Order at St. Michael's Mount, however, was to remain due to its importance strategically in the guardianship of its port. Otherwise much damage, stripping down, and selling of monastic lands and buildings proceeded. This was to achieve, without the necessary intention to do so, a completely new social order. And despite comments made by the King's Librarian, Leland, in 1538, about the priests being absent most of the time, the deanery of St. Buryan remained for another three centuries. The clergy were made to abandon their residences, and these were sold to gentry and merchants who could afford to extend and re-build or even build anew on ecclesiastical estates. A general re-distribution of tithes and other incomes followed, and in this way the Duchy (the Earldom of Cornwall, bestowed on the King's eldest son) also extended its ownership of lands. A new elite for Cornwall was created. Whereas most of the lands of the Earldom of Cornwall had been in the eastern part of the county, now more was pulled in from the west to the Duchy, particularly the Isles of Scilly. Today (in AD 2000), Charles, Duke of Cornwall, continues in that ownership.

In general, and certainly following the so-called 'Prayer Book Rebellion', the loyalty of the Cornish gentry, those who had also gained personally from the dissolution of monastic lands, was again rewarded. From this era began the new chartering of towns in Cornwall, and the creation of an over-abundance of Parliamentary seats, the source of the term 'the rotten boroughs'. At one time, Cornwall was returning 44 members to Parliament, most of whom spent little time if any in Cornwall. The commissioner located in west Cornwall in the 16th C. was Sir William Godolphin, and the fact of his family seat between Penzance and Helston was to prove of greatest importance to Penzance and other settlements of Mount's Bay. But, first the battle, then the spoils!

The 'Prayer Book Rebellion'
Several changes in religious practice contributed to the next rebellion in Cornwall, and it was at parish level that the people could see and feel them. First, in 1548, orders were received, via overseers (agents of the King and parliament), that images were to be removed from all churches and chapels. Popish practices such as the use of elaborate vestments, incense and ashes in Christian festivals, were to be stopped. Holy Bread and Holy Water were not to be used and candles for worship at chapels abandoned.

One such overseer, William Body, was busy destroying the images in Helston church, when an angry mob of a thousand men following the lead of a priest of St. Keverne, pulled him out into the street and killed him. A revolt was imminent, but justices from east Cornwall managed to catch the murderers, and see to it that they were hung, drawn and quartered. The priest, not unlike An Gof, was executed in London, and the others in Launceston. But this was not to be the end of it.

Parliament passed the 'Act of Uniformity' in January of 1549, making it compulsory for the people to use the *Book of Common Prayer* in English, rather than the Latin Mass and services known to them. After the Prayer Book was first introduced at Whitsun, and a movement back to the Latin Mass had begun in Devon, it was only a few days before revolt was in the air again at Bodmin. Some of the gentry who opposed the rebellion retreated to castles. In west Cornwall some were to shut themselves into St. Michael's Mount, where rebels forced their surrender by denying them food, and besieging them with burning trusses of hay. Though no casualties occurred here, this was just the beginning.

Rallying around the mayor of Bodmin, Henry Bray, and two local gentry of staunch Catholic belief, once again, thousands proceeded into Devon to join up with the rebels there and head for Exeter. Though there were sympathies for the rebels at Exeter, their memories were long enough to recall the ultimate failure of each of the two previous Cornish debacles. So, a siege began which kept Exeter locked within its gates for five weeks. Lord Russell was sent with troops for the Crown and was later joined by Lord Grey together with Italian and German mercenaries. It was only after savage fighting with many losses that the rebels fled, re-grouped and lost again.

Meantime, they had put their demands in a petition to King Edward VI (Henry VIII having died in 1547). They wanted the return of the Old Latin service with all the ritual they were used to. The Cornish in particular had a strong case: they could not understand the *New Prayer Book*, not that they 'understood' Latin as such, and most were illiterate.

"...we will have our old service of Mattins, Mass, Evensong and Procession in Latin as it was before. And so we the Cornish men whereof certain of us understand no English utterly refuse this new English."

There was to be no acceptance of such reasoning on the part of the new Church of England. The aftermath of the rebellion was horrible indeed. The leaders, including Catholics Arundell and Winslade, were hung and cut to pieces, the Devonshire men waving on gibbets like flags from Dunster to Bath. Priests, including the then vicar of Gulval near Penzance, were also executed and hundreds were wounded and killed in battle.

Frank Halliday summarises how this affected daily lives:
"A second and more uncompromisingly Protestant Prayer Book [in English] was introduced, and non-attendance at church punished with imprisonment. The clergy were allowed to marry, more images were removed and more lights extinguished in the churches, while the stone altars of the Mass were carried out and wooden tables for communion carried in. Commissions were appointed to assess and seize the now superfluous apparatus of candlesticks, crosses, censers and so on, one chalice for communion and one bell to summon

communicants being all that the needy government considered necessary for a normal church."

Then Edward VI died, and Catholic Mary (daughter of Henry VIII and Katherine of Aragon) was made Queen. All was to return as it had been before! Another paragraph from Halliday:

"The Prayer Book was abolished, the Latin Mass restored; the wooden communion tables were carried out, the stone altars carried in; the confiscated apparatus of candlesticks, crosses and so on were needed...now there were to be no more married clergy. Those who had married in Edward's reign were offered the choice between their wives and their benefices... Most chose their benefices."

Mary I, despite plots and plans in which West Country grandees and pirates played roles, lasted only five years on the throne. It was then 'all change' as Elizabeth I began her long reign in 1558. Elizabeth's policy was to revert to the Protestant order of things, and to make it as easy as possible for this to happen. With hardly a whisper of complaint, English became the language of religious service.

Spoken language and its reform

In Cornwall, the religious reforms marked the beginning of the slow but sure decline of Cornish as the natural speaking language of the people. There had never been a Cornish version of the Bible, and gradually the Cornish ear adjusted itself to the sounds of the new tongue. Naturally, as before mentioned, the language shift was to happen in the east of Cornwall faster than in the west. Within West Cornwall itself, English was taken on more easily and quickly in Penzance and in St. Ives, than in the country. And, the use of English also spread down from the landowners, who had the opportunities both to travel abroad and to educate

DOROTHY PENTREATH of MOUSEHOLE in CORNWALL

themselves, to the working classes who could do neither. By 1700 only the least educated retained knowledge of the language. Much is made in

Mousehole's history of the supposed last Cornish speaker (who used it in daily conversation), Dorothy Rawlings or as also known 'Dolly Pentreath', and a plaque is on her house there. Others dispute the claim.

The age of mining arrives
In these years, a major change in methods of exploiting metal and mineral resource was taking place in Cornwall. Tin streams were exhausted, and the only means of obtaining the ores was to dig for them. Of particular importance in the industry was Sir William Godolphin, whose estates between Helston and Penzance, were rich in tin. When young Leland had surveyed in 1538 as mentioned above, Godolphin's holdings were the largest in Cornwall.

William died in 1575, and his stake in tin and copper working, devolved to his nephew and heir Sir Francis, who devoted his life to the trade. Up to 300 men worked for him in Penwith and Kerrier districts, and even German mining engineers were imported for their skills in extracting underground ore. The truth was that mining was now becoming more expensive overall in Cornwall, because the deeper it became, the more it cost in equipment, in time, and naturally, the toll it took on the lives of the working miners. It had also become more expensive than small associations of miners could afford, so the age of capitalist mining companies had arrived. Inevitably this would also mean that Cornishmen would begin, in larger numbers, though this was still a little way ahead, to look around for other mining opportunities in other lands. There were already Cornish miners in Brittany in some number and in Spain, and of course, west Cornwall had its face to the sea where visitors came and went on a frequent basis. They would hear where their best chances were to get work, wherever that would take them.

The Spanish Raids of 1595
Queen Mary in the 1550s had married Philip of Spain, and this had underlined her Catholic loyalties. The exiled Killigrew brothers of Cornwall (Falmouth), in parallel, had begun a life of privateering and piracy on the

high seas, their main targets being Spanish ships. One they sank off the Land's End, stealing her cargo, putting it into Scilly as a base. Though Elizabeth I was crowned in 1558, in good relations with Spain, piracy and plundering continued, made worse by Spanish counter-attacks. Within a decade this meant very unfriendly relations, if not outright war.

In 1568, one John Hawkins, a slave trader, put into Mount's Bay with one of his original six ships, his cousin Francis Drake arriving at Plymouth with another. They had abandoned a hundred of their men to the mercy of the Spaniards and according to reports, the English who were not killed out-right by the Spanish were sent to the Inquisition. The victims had not been charged as smugglers, which they were, but heretics! Growing anti-Spanish feeling was added to in England by a renewed anti-Catholic attitude.

The long spate of sea skirmishes with the Spanish continued, most of which did not touch the people of Cornwall in any respect. But as full-scale war approached with the threat of the Spanish Armada, Cornwall was England's most important outpost. Though invasion was also planned from the coast of the Netherlands, in the first instance, the invaders too would have to sail past the western coastal region.

Sir Francis Drake with a foray to Cadiz managed to delay the Armada for a year, but finally in summer of 1588, the Spanish fleet of nearly 150 ships sailed along the Cornish Coast, past Land's End and further east toward Plymouth. A combination of bad weather and smaller, faster boats on the part of the English defenders, sent the Spanish back to Spain with only about half of their ships. Counter attacks followed, but by 1590 the whole strategy of the Spanish changed, which endangered the Cornish much more.

The Spaniards occupied Brittany, supporting the Catholics in the French Civil War, and for eight years would have a base for hassling Cornwall. And, so to July of 1595 when completely surprising the people of Mousehole, four Spanish galleons sailed into the bay and landed up to 200 men with pikes and shot. They proceeded to spread out and burn everything within half a mile of the village including the parish church of Paul, and then return to burn and ravage Mousehole itself. The vicar of Paul at the time was John Tremearne, and later the Tremearnes married into the Branwell family (the maternal inheritance line of the famed Bronte sisters).

Sir Francis Godolphin observed the smoke of the firing as he was riding towards Penzance and galloped instead to Mousehole with his servants, rallying the fleeing residents as he went. He thought the invasion had finally come, and he took the precaution of sending immediately by post to Plymouth to warn Drake and Hawkins, and asking for any help they could spare. With whatever few weapons they could muster, some hundred Cornish gathered on a green at the west side of Penzance and prepared to advance on the enemy still at Mousehole. Almost as suddenly as they landed, the Spanish re-embarked and came along the coast a little, landing their entire force of some 400 men at Newlyn.

It was 4 to 1 in favour of the Spanish, and Godolphin with a straggling, frightened few -- by this time mainly his own servants (barely a dozen he reported) -- tried to make a stand at the marketplace in Penzance. The rest had fled through fear. All had been forced to leave Newlyn, and then Penzance behind, both to be fired by the advancing Spaniards. And now we have the last part of his report from Goldolphin, as rendered in modern English by Halliday:

"By this time, towards the evening, the Cornish forces, increased in number and amended in heart, encamped themselves on the green near to the town of Markasiew (Marazion) and St. Michael's Mount for the defence thereof, and there spent the night. The next day the enemy made show to land again on the west side of the bay, but seeing the people, though few in number yet resolute to resist, they desisted from their enterprise and besides, finding themselves annoyed by the shooting of bullets and arrows into their galleys, where they rode at anchor, they were forced to remove them farther off."

The following day the Spaniards unloaded some English prisoners whom they had been keeping on one of the galleys. One of these, an Ipswich man, told Godolphin that the Spaniards had been helped and guided by a rebel Englishman of Dorset, and that the Spanish would have stayed longer if they had not been so frightened of the coming of Drake and his force from Plymouth. The prisoner also said that "after they had burned Penzance and other villages they had a Mass next day on the western hill, where they vowed to found a friary when they had conquered England."

Keigwin at Mousehole, drawn by D Stephenson for 'The Paper Chase', 1909

Amongst the three that were killed was Jenken Keigwin of Mousehole. What any visitor to Mousehole today can still see is his home, Keigwin, perhaps the only house of consequence to have survived the Spanish raid. Actual casualties were few, and it was said by many afterwards that lives were only saved because the people ran away. Godolphin was certainly the hero of the day, and a few gentlemen stood firm with him. In smoking ruins were Mousehole, Newlyn, and Penzance. Only Marazion stood unharmed because the invaders never got that far.

That same year, 1595, Marazion was to receive its charter of incorporation as a borough. As a town it seemed to try with that position to 'do down' the rest of the Mount's Bay area. Whereas the Penzance traders began to hold an unauthorised Saturday market to resurrect trade after the Spanish raid, the Corporation of Marazion tried to stop them and finally took them to court for running an illegal enterprise. This was only an early example of how economic regeneration is hard to pull off in a small set of communities where one group's livelihood is easily threatened by another's, and everyone is watching every move. Though, in the end, Marazion won its case in 1604, sympathy for damages caused to Penzance by the Spanish invasion were expressed by the Court. Ten years later, in 1614, the town of Penzance, complete with its Charter from James I, became a Borough. Then it was truly in control of its own affairs.

Carew's Survey of Cornwall 1602 & Fiennes' Diary of 1698
The main source of our knowledge about the Cornwall of the Elizabethan era comes from the master work of Richard Carew, which is not only a social and industrial survey, but an important piece of literature in its own right. He completed and published it in the year before Elizabeth's reign came to an end, and James I was to ascend the throne.

Though he says little about Penzance as a place, his descriptions of fishing, farming and mining are important to our understanding of the methods used at this period. He tells about pilchards and how they are packed. He tells about nets and how they were used with what kinds of boats. He mentions that fishermen may also be miners, and still do a bit of farming on the side. Though certainly a member of the gentry himself, he observes certain improvements in the lives of the working population. Some have windows in their cottages, some wooden floorboards on which they walk.

He noted harvest festivals, and the fact that there is more fun in life than there used to be!

He projects an interesting picture, but one that cannot be related in just a few words. But, he is worth reading, just as the diary of Celia Fiennes, who made her famous horseback journey through Cornwall in the autumn of 1698. At the end of an eventful 17th C. she again describes the mines, how they were worked and how drained, how rough she found the muddy roads, and how smooth and sweet the cream she was fed.

Penzance, a chartered town
The Charter under which Penzance was to be administratively governed for more than two centuries, was first granted by James I in 1614. The leadership appointed were to be a Mayor, eight Aldermen and twelve Councillors who were called Assistants. Those appointed are named in full, and selected for life, with only the future Mayors to be voted from the Aldermen on an annual basis.

THE PENZANCE MARKET CROSS 1836.

This was in fact a closed system, and vacancies by death were filled from the rung below to the Alderman rank, and from upright citizens to the Assistant level. The ordinary Townsperson had no voice in the selection, and this was the common pattern of the time.

The town was defined by a circle of half-mile radius from the Market Cross that stood at the centre of four roads in the Green Market. That Market Cross now stands in Penlee Park, near the entrance to the Penlee Art Gallery and Museum, where it was re-positioned in autumn, 1997. (Its seventh position in the town)

The rights and duties specified are detailed in the Charter, a copy of which is reprinted in Peter Pool's *History of the Town and Borough of Penzance*. Space does not allow for their repetition here. But, an important part grants the rights for two weekly markets, on Tuesdays and Thursdays, replacing the single market held on Wednesdays to that time, and also the allowance for seven fairs of various lengths of days.

The old borough seal of Penzance bearing the head of John the Baptist

In 1615, the Penzance Corporation bought a plot of land from the then owner of the Manor of Alverton, Richard Daniell (a Truro merchant of standing), upon which was constructed a Market House and Guildhall. Five years later, the town seal that was also authorised by the Charter, was adopted and entered in the heraldic register. That seal, a 'logo' of considerable artistic merit, if rather morbid style, is reprinted here, and depicts St. John the Baptist's head on a platter. It is clearly a visual reference to, perhaps a very clever pun on, the name of Penzance.

The English Civil War and Penzance
At its simplest the English Civil War was an almighty fight between the King, with his Royalist supporters, and the Parliament, and its backers, over who should direct the fortunes and the future of the country. The economic, religious, and cultural sides to this are complex and sometimes confusing due to the fact that various factions and individual leaders changed sides from time to time. So while the Civil War certainly split counties, factions within counties, and even families, there was a mix and match of a high order in the political and religious hierarchies that determined how daily life was managed.

In Cornwall, piracy was continuing and defences had been neglected. Privateers working out of the French coast at Dunkirk persistently preyed on English shipping. Even worse were the Mohammedan pirates (usually known as the 'Barbary Corsairs') from Morocco who in long, very fast ships constantly raided the coast carrying off people into 'the white slave trade'. In one ten day period in 1625, 27 ships and 200 men were taken by pirates. A few weeks earlier 60 men, women and children had been grabbed out of a Mount's Bay church. As Halliday puts it "No wonder the people of Penzance were so 'terribly terrified by the Turks' that they petitioned the Council for a fort to protect them."

Embedded in the Cornish person, despite awareness of economic deprivation and political abuse, was, and possibly still is, a deep conservatism, and resistance to change. Whereas only a century before they had revolted against the Anglican Church and its bringing of the 'Sawsen' (Saxon) tongue, now in the 1640s their loyalties were mainly to the Royalist cause. The Parliamentarians, fair as they might wish to be, would nevertheless project too many changes in whatever direction.

In the West Country it was to be primarily a fight between the Devonians for Parliament and the Cornish for the King, who was, of course, the fateful Charles I. In the fearsome battles, the Cornish consistently won the battles but lost massively, not only leaders of stature of Grenville, Godolphin (Sydney, a poet and soldier), Trevanion, Slanning, but more than half of their foot soldiers. And writers compared it to the break-up of the fellowship of the Round Table, an echo of Arthurian romance.

The importance of Cornwall to the King was as a recruiting ground for the Royalists. He could draw upon tin revenue to finance his forces and their provisions. The Royalist strongholds were falling by 1645, when Sir Arthur Basset finally surrendered St. Michael's Mount after long and bloody battles, moving further west all the time. Meantime, the Prince of Wales with 300 Royalist supporters had been encamped on Scilly, and on the same day as the Mount was given over to the Parliamentary forces, the Royalists left Scilly for Jersey, and from there by summer the whole were exiles in France. The Civil War in Cornwall was over, but change was the order. Though two further uprisings occurred in Penzance, causing the Parliamentary troops to rally and turn on them, the plague finally put an end to resistence. For two years following the war the death toll rose dramatically.

The clergy and the churches suffered badly from the Puritan reformers. The Anglican clergy were driven from their homes with their families, more than a hundred in Cornwall losing their livings and receiving no pensions. Whatever the reformation had not destroyed, the Puritan reformers would mop up. Men were paid to smash any stained glass remaining.

A final paragraph from Halliday graphically sums up the 'leftovers' for Cornwall:

"...the Cornish people as a whole were in a pitiful condition. Apart from the loss of many of their best men, they had suffered the depredations of invading armies...harvests had been lost, tin mines flooded and bridges broken; and now they had to support an army of bureaucrats busily collecting taxes and fines. To make matters worse the end of the war was followed by bad harvest, and plague...St. Ives was isolated and, though food from neighbouring parishes was placed on the boundary of the stricken area, more than five hundred people, about a third of the population, died of famine and pestilence." Out of this disastrous Civil War, would have to come reconstruction, and over the following two decades moves in that direction would be made.

The Mount was sold by the Bassets, who were Royalist losers, to John St. Aubyn of Clowance (near Helston), the Parliamentary leader in 1657. Since that day the Mount has stayed in the benevolent hands of the St. Aubyn family, as it does today with the supportive protection of the National Trust.

Coinage, stannaries, and taxation

Since medieval times there had been 'coinage' centres for the Stannaries (the four geographical mining districts of Cornwall). These were established under Charter by King John in 1201 to separate them from the stannaries in Devon. The sources for the principles and 'rules' under which mining could take place and who could do it appear to be several, based on Anglo-Saxon, Norman and Cornish 'common law' as it evolved through centuries. In the 14th C. further charters defined rights and priveleges for the tinners, and set up the framework of law courts applying to them, employment and self-employment opportunities, as well as their Stannary Parliament, not unlike the Parliament for the whole of the country, but just for Cornwall.

The original coinage centres, where tin was weighed, identified by source, and taxed for the Duchy benefit, were designated as Liskeard, Lostwithiel, Truro and Helston. In 1663, in a Crown petition, the people of Penzance asked for this status as well. The centre of tin operations was moving from the east to the west, and Helston was inconvenient for the tinners of Penwith as its gross weights increased. It was expensive for the trade to haul it to Helston for taxation purposes. The Charter granted, a new coinage hall was built at town expense, attached to the market house (just below) at the top of Market Jew Street. There it remained until 1816, when a new one was built near the quay, more convenient for shipping out the taxed tin.

The advantage of becoming a coinage town to Penzance was great: port facilities would be supported and extended, and in the long term, the establishment of the town as an administrative centre for the tin trade was beneficial. This was a good example of 'people power', and enterprise on the part of the Town fathers. Other coinage towns resented losing part of their trade, and from time to time, tried to discourage use of Penzance's chartered powers. But, the blowing-house for treatment of tin ore at Chyandour, then on the edge of Penzance proper, was the only one operating in Penwith at that time. It was to become a chief smelting house for Cornwall.

In legend and literature
Culturally, the most dramatic change occurring in Penzance during this phase was the shift from Cornish to English. The process was not a simple one, and cannot be put down as a straightforward 'decline' from East to West. Considering Penzance's role as a port, one might expect the language to have altered here first. However, Penzance and west Cornwall in particular remained a stronghold of Cornish for a considerable time. Indeed, there was in Penzance, quite a frantic burst of activity to make sure that knowledge of Cornish remained and much detail of its grammar, vocabulary and literature should be both revived and preserved.

One of the more famous texts of this period of Cornish literature, is *John of Chyanhor* by Nicholas Boson (c.1665). The tale revolves around three points of wisdom:
'Do not leave an old way for a new way'
'Do not lodge in a house where an old man may be married to a young woman'
'Be struck twice before you strike once, for that is best point of wit of all'.
Boson first heard the story from some of his family's servants, indicating that instead of Cornish language being marginalised, it was actually a vehicle

for some of the major European folk narratives.

John Boson was the son of Nicholas Boson, and he composed an astonish-
ing poem called 'The Pilchard Curing Rhyme' which demonstrates the
importance of pilchard fishing and production in Penzance. Boson takes the
reader though all the processes of curing, storing and packing the fish,
emphasising the social cohesion required to sustain the industry. The scene
in the opening of the poem is particularly vivid showing all the activity as
the boats come in:

> *My song is on pilchards with boat and net
> Taken in the bay of the Grey Rock in the Wood.
> When the boats had come home
> From the sea people cried, "Tithe! Tithe!"
> And every woman near to her husband
> With a basket and three hundred pilchards on her back.
> To make smoked pilchards in every house
> With mouth wide open, "Pilchards! Pilchards! More salt!

The final lines show how pilchard products were exported to the
Mediterranean, in the light of Lent and other fasts in Roman Catholic
countries. The faithful there were enjoined to abstain from meat; thus
sustaining the Penzance pilchard industry:

> *At last, the wind of the North East will blow far
> For the people of hot countries will eat them all.
> The wealth of pilchards is like all the world
> More poor people than rich people.

*Originally written in Cornish, the above poems have been translated by Tim Saunders and
Alan Kent. Reprinted here, with permission, from their book listed in the Reading Trail for
Chapter 2.

Another important scholar of the language was James Jenkins of Alverton,
Penzance. Sadly, very little remains of James Jenkins' poetry and yet he was

regarded by his contemporaries as one of the most learned Cornish writers. I have included this one poem in the original Cornish with its translation beside. This poem, written with internal rhyme, offers us advice about women, relationships and life:

> Ma leeaz Greage. Lacka vel Zeage.
> Gwel gerres. Vell commerez.
> Ha ma leeaz Bennen. Pocare an Gwennen.
> Eye vedn gwrrez de gu Teez. Dandle peath an beaz.
> Fleaz hep skeeanz. Vedn gweel gu Seeaznz.
> Bur mor crown gy pedery. Pan dall gu gwary.
> Ha madra ta. Pandrigg Seera ha Damah.
> Narehanz moaz dan Cooz. Do cuntle gu booz.
> Buz gen nebbes lavirrians. Eye venjah dendel gu booz dillaz.
>
> [There are many wives worse than chaff,
> Better left than taken,
> And there are many women like the bees,
> They will help their men to earn worldly wealth.
> Children without wisdom will do their whim,
> But if they think what their play is worth
> And take careful note of what father and mother did
> They would not go to the wood to collect their food
> But with a little labour they would earn their food and drink.]

Such poems capture much about the people of Penzance and their attitudes toward life and society during this period. William Gwavas was another one of the most important scholars and writers of Cornish. He was born in 1676 and became a barrister of the Middle Temple in London, where he lived for some time in Brickcourt, Westminster. He died in 1741 and is buried at Paul. Penzance and the Mount's Bay area were inspirational to him and figure in his imagery.

Late Cornish poetry is totally without mention of God and religion, and this is a major change from the Middle-Cornish of the Miracle plays. Cornish-speaking people had been strongly alienated by the reform of their celtic-catholicism into a 'Church of England' and believed it to be 'foreign' to their culture.

For many people, the sheer toil of scratching a living, and the seemingly endless revisions of their religious practice, served to drive them away from religion altogether. And, from the Reformation, there was a new division which emerged between the Anglo-Cornish who considered themselves English and would be educated as such, and those who considered that Cornwall was its own land sufficient to itself. That tension, to some degree but often in good humour and jest, can still be observed today.

Perhaps the final words may be given to William Gwavas, who in 1721, wrote the following poem, referring as it does to Penzance's geography and the flooding of Mounts Bay:

> This Towne on Riseing Ground doth stand,
> Bounded with distant Hills to Land,
> And southward shutes into the Sea,
> Where lies for Shipping a Good Key.
> In prospect of the famous Mount
> That stands in the Sea, tho' by Account
> In Antient Brittish Times it stood
> A vinew'd Rock, within a Wood.

The Reading Trail for Chapter 2

R. Pearse Chope, Editor (1918 repr. 1967 with a new introduction by Alan Gibson) *Early Tours in Devon and Cornwall*, David & Charles: Newton Abbot.

F.E. Halliday , Editor (1969) *Richard Carew of Antony: The Survey of Cornwall*, Andrew Melrose for Social Documents Ltd.: London.

 (1959) *A History of Cornwall*, London: Gerald Duckworth & Co.

Alan M. Kent and Tim Saunders, Editors and translators, (2000) *Looking at the Mermaid: A Reader in Cornish Literature 900-1900*, London: Francis Boutle.

Alan M. Kent (ed.), *Voices from West Barbary: An Anthology of Anglo-Cornish Poetry 1549-1928*, (2000) London: Francis Boutle.

Philip Payton (1996) *Cornwall*, Fowey: Alexander Associates.

Charles Thomas (1999) *Penzance Market Cross: A Cornish Wonder Re-Wondered*, Penzance: Penlee House.

CHAPTER 3

PENZANCE AND THE INDUSTRIAL AGE 1720-1900

The 18th and 19th centuries was a period of growth and prosperity, the like of which Penzance had not known before and has not since. The roots of it may be traced to the strength and resourcefulness of the people in overcoming the distress and destruction of the civil war conflicts, and also through the increased scientific, political and cultural participation of west Cornish people in the affairs of the nation.

From the start of the 1700s there are many more stories to be told and many more tellers of the tale. Records in the form of town and court documents, newspapers, and personal papers of important local gentry come into play, some of which confirm each other, some of which don't even agree as to date and place. It becomes harder to summarise because there is always a different story for the wealthy and the poor, for the farmers and the fishermen, for the educated gentry and the illiterate labourers, for those energised by a new evangelical movement, and those rejecting it for one reason or another. Not least throughout the 18th and 19th centuries, are the many different stories of migrants who come into West Cornwall to live and work, settling in and around Penzance, and those who leave to make a life elsewhere.

Opening the doors
Perhaps the best analogy is one to do with doors; the doors to Cornwall

have always been open to emigrants who have come and stayed. From earliest times people came, and survived here through the traditional means of supporting themselves: fishing, farming and streaming for metals. In the 18th and 19th centuries the balance was to change radically, and the doors were to become the more modern revolving ones. Penzance, like its neighbours around the Bay, was built with the sea (and its trades) at its front door; in the next two centuries the front door opened onto land. As land-based transport became more efficient, a two-way traffic through the revolving door became the natural order of the day. Penzance became the Land's End terminus of the railway in 1852, and with that change -- in which Cornish inventors of genius took full part -- the doors were propped permanently open.

The elements of the Revolution
In the 18th C. a new age was being entered, though people in the daily grind of their lives, would not have realised it at the time. This was to be the new 'industrial age', or as popularly now entitled 'the Industrial Revolution'. Great wealth was to come to Cornwall but, nevertheless, only a few would benefit and much would be taken elsewhere to shareholders and venture capitalists.

The experience gained in hard-rock mining by Cornish miners would mean that they were courted by the world. In good times they were recruited for their experience, and in bad times at home, they would seek employment elsewhere. Naturally the changes did not happen in a day or a week or a year, and many factors contributed to the network of activities and inventions that were to change lives forever. Nor were changes confined to Penzance, or the Land's End area, as any student of the Industrial Revolution knows, and this is an important point. What will be described here is only the way in which the elements of major revolutions (for there were many as technology progressed) were reflected in West Cornwall life but they are not confined to one geographical place.
The natural resources of Cornwall, tin, copper, minerals, china clay, ensured that the Cornish were partners in the enterprise which was forwarded in

several key places in Britain. And, the position of Cornishmen in key roles nationally, helping to shape the new age for Britain and its colonies, is a record in which to take pride. These dual resources -- its natural ones and its human ones -- make up the story of the Land's End district as well as that of its commercial and trade centre, Penzance.

A change from what?
Halliday begins his own story of Cornwall at the beginning of the 1700s with the following summary:

"...remote and still barely accessible save to the hardy adventurer, its people pursued their own peculiar way of life, preserving their Celtic legends, festivals and folklore, and in the far west even their own language. It was still a foreign country with a culture of its own, and even if its independent political history was finished [i.e. it was now very much a part of England politically], its distinctive economic history was not; indeed, it might be argued that it was only just beginning. Geologically the county was unique; no other region in Britain had a comparable wealth of metal below its surface, and as yet it had scarcely been worked. The next two centuries of the history of Cornwall, therefore, are essentially the history of its mining industry."

What visitors observed
Between the visits of the two now famous travellers, Fiennes and Defoe, briefly described here, a great deal was happening in West Cornwall. Around the early 1700s began the transformation that produced the physical place of the Penzance we would recognise today. Stemming from the same four lanes, centred on the tri-cornered plot of the Market House and the original Coinage Hall (now housing a Bank and several shops at upper and lower levels) the growth of the town can be plotted in detail from the maps and records available. The lanes, now the streets, are, of course, those of Chapel Street leading up from the harbour, Causewayhead leading down from the north, Alverton Street leading in from the west, and Market Jew leading in from Chyandour and Marazion on the eastern side of the town.

A wide-ranging account of historical developments in cultural topics from architecture to crime to religion and education in Penzance leading up to and through the Napoleonic war period (from approximately 1750-1815), is published in 2000 by the Penwith Local History Group. For the interested reader, wanting greater detail on subjects than can be summarised here, *In and around Penzance during Napoleonic Times*, is highly recommended. June Palmer introduces this book by pointing to the end of the 18th C. and the beginning of the 19th C. as "a very special period in the history of Cornwall." Her reasons for saying this are particularly appropriate:

"Before this time Cornwall had always been perceived by those who lived elsewhere in the country as a rather outlandish place, remote from London. At the end of the eighteenth century these perceptions were to change. The expansion of the road system, due to the creation of the Turnpike Trusts, brought Cornwall within much easier reach of London and many took the opportunity to visit the county...". As early as 1747, the *Sherborne Mercury* (Dorset) for example, listed properties for sale and let, and hotels and inns for the traveller in Penzance were noted. Within 50 years more local newspapers were to appear, *The Royal Cornwall Gazette* and *The West Briton* (1810), and take over coverage of the whole of Cornwall. *The Cornishman*, focusing on West Cornwall, did not begin until the 1870s, but it continues to this day linked to other regional newspapers printed at Plymouth (*Western Morning News* Group).

In 1803, after attending a play in London, which purported to be set in Penzance, Valentine Le Grice wrote the following letter to the *Royal Cornwall Gazette*:

"Imagine my surprise at finding the vicinity of Penzance represented as a desert moor...I know that an idea prevails, that around Penzance every wind that blows is a storm, that the few houses which are above ground are built of wrecked timber, that the underground inhabitants are the most numerous, that the above-ground gentlemen are all smugglers, and that every horse at night is a kind of will o'whisp, and carries a lantern at his tail to decoy the coasting mariner. Now I beg leave to inform Mr. Colman* that Penzance is a very different place from the commonly received opinion. We have cards for the sedentary, books for the lounger, balls for the light-heeled, clubs for the convivial, and picnics..." [*Mr. Colman was the playwright!]

Even with the turnpikes, however, achieving Penzance by road was not quick, even though coming overland to Launceston at the eastern end of the county was made easier from points east. By 1760 a turnpike road existed between Penryn (Falmouth) and Marazion, just three miles from Penzance. By 1805, it was definitely thought faster to travel by post-chaise from Falmouth to London, to bring news of Trafalgar, rather than get there by sea. But, Penzance heard sooner and, in fact, first on the mainland of Britain, if the legend is to be trusted. The story is HMS Pickle returning with the news of the loss of Nelson on its way in to Falmouth harbour, passed a Penzance fishing boat, and shared the information. The fishermen rushed to the Mayor, Thomas Giddy, attending a ball in the Union Hotel at the time. From the minstrel gallery there, he was said to have made that announcement, and promised a memorial service at nearby Madron Parish Church, which followed soon after.

Communication links and trade routes increased steadily throughout this period, spurred on by the needs of the industrial drive. Boats left Hayle regularly for South Wales and Bristol, for the export of minerals and the import of coal, and there were boats to Plymouth, London and France from the southern ports of Penzance, Marazion, and Falmouth. On all of these the people associated with industrial development travelled. Within Cornwall, most commonly, provisions were moved by packhorse, and individuals travelled by horseback along bridle paths and rocky lanes.

A wealth of metal
Celia Fiennes on her horseback ride through Cornwall, saw and described the tinning and smelting process of the time (1698). In several places in her account she mentions the lack of coal and wood, and the restrictions this placed on treatments for metals locally. She observed, too, what was one of the greatest difficulties encountered in mining labour: the flooding of the shafts as they drove deeper into the lodes. But in that same year a start had been made on trying to solve this problem by Captain Thomas Savery with his pumping device. Based on the principle of a steam engine, it was designed to draw water out of Cornish mines.

Working later with a Devon blacksmith, Thomas Newcomen, Savery was to help devise the beam engine that was first employed in Cornish mines in 1712. The age of steam had arrived, but the need now was for large amounts of fuel -- coal or wood -- to feed the 'firing engines' for smelting. Since Cornwall had little natural fuel, this was a problem that brought shippers and merchants, and more labourers, into the wider spread of employment related to mining. Important now was the price of coal, if Cornwall was not to be completely stripped of its wood. And in this, another Godolphin was to help his native land.

Of particular importance in the period of Queen Anne (1702-1714) was the Cornishman, Sidney Godolphin, the nephew of the Royalist Cavalier poet killed in the Civil War and MP for Helston. This Godolphin, brought up in the Royal Court, was to become Lord Treasurer for the Crown, and to play the politically significant role of negotiator for the coming together of England and Scotland in the Act of Union, 1707. During his tenure in office, the price of tin was raised by at least a third, and he secured a lowering of the duty to be paid on the coal imported to Cornwall that was used in smelting. This was a beginning, but there was much more invention to come from the Cornish.

A well set-up town
When Daniel Defoe published the record of his tour through Great Britain in 1724, his comments about Penzance were positive:
"...a place of good business, well built and populous, has a good trade, and a great many ships belonging to it, notwithstanding it is so remote. Here are also a great many good families of gentlemen, though in this utmost angle of the nation; and which is yet more strange, the veins of lead, tin, and copper ore are said to be seen even to the utmost extent of land at low-water mark, and in the very sea--so rich, so valuable, a treasure is contained in these parts of Great Britain, though they are supposed to be so poor, because so very remote from London..."

In fact, Defoe's words were more forward-looking than he would know in relation to metals and the sea. Some fifty years later (1778) a business man of Breage sunk a shaft in a reef between Newlyn and Penzance at the location now called Wherrytown (the site of two supermarkets and a model boating lake in 2000), calling it the Wherry Mine. This was the only major mine in the immediate vicinity of Penzance itself, and it continued working until 1798, when an American ship, cutting adrift from its moorings, demolished its structure. Finally, after several attempts to make it work again, it closed forever in 1840. Within short distances of the town, of course, working mines were in evidence, the famed Ding Dong Mine between Madron and Newmill being a prime example, and that would not close until the 1870s.

Though mining for tin and even more profitably for copper was centred elsewhere (St. Just in Penwith for west Cornwall) Penzance, in particular, benefited greatly from its position as a coinage town. The money to be gained in mining was in owning the estates to be mined, and in the ownership of the smelting and treatment works. After the coinage dues were collected according to weight and the ingots were stamped, the port for shipping tin to London was readily available. The stannary laws governing the transport from the coinage hall to the pier were both specific and strict in fear of tax evasion (which robbed the King!). One rule, for example, was that the tin should be transported in the middle of the day; anyone found transporting it by night, therefore, would be known to be 'up to something'.

Before being abolished in 1838, coinage responsibilities had established the trading and market importance of the town of Penzance. By this time the coinage hall had been removed from the Market House, and in 1816 put in a new building down by the quay, very near the site of the original St. Anthony's Chapel. The original coinage activities, however, by increasing the economic and financial aspects of the town automatically supported the fishing market and trades, animal husbandry and agriculture. Before touching the subjects of fishing and farming, however, let us review the physical condition of Penzance and its district in the early 1700s.

Visions and re-visions for Market House, Penzance.
Now Sir Humphry Davy stands in front.

The 'New Town' of Penzance

The re-building of both Penzance and Mousehole after the Spanish sackings in 1595, appears to have been taken up quite quickly, if the Town Charter of 1614 is to be believed. Nevertheless, Penzance was roughly treated twice more, if not destroyed completely, in 1646-48 following the Civil War, first by the Parliamentary troops under Sir Thomas Fairfax and later, Colonel Bennett. The west Cornish people were known to have been Royalist in sympathies, and troublesome in nature. Because of the destruction, and also due to plague at the same time, the population was decimated (up to a third of men, women and children). Left with few energies and resources, there are few buildings in town which can definitely be dated to the 1600s....though, there are features within buildings, especially on Chapel Street, which hark back as far as Tudor times. A chimney stack here, a Tudor fireplace there, a wall here and there.

Because of these factors, Penzance, by re-building would become a 'new town' in the latter part of the 17th C. In the new century and with fortunes made through mining and related businesses (such as coinage and banking), the larger, finer residences now sitting around the outer periphery of Penzance were constructed and inhabited. Fine houses were also reconstructed, built anew, and improved, especially lining Chapel Street leading down to the harbour.

Most of the 18th C. history of the place, Penzance, was played out from the Market House down Chapel Street to the quay. The social centre was the Ship and Castle Inn (earliest newspaper reference: 1747, as the house of Samuel Bennetts, innkeeper), and the homes of the wealthiest and most influential of its families. Chapel Street was also the religious centre with St. Mary's Chapel near the bottom, and the commercial and professional centre with the Market House at the top. The Post Office, which now is located on Market Jew Street, was also located in two separate places on Chapel Street. This was probably to be near the Ship and Castle Inn, where the post-chaise came and went, not only with post but with road passengers in the later years of the century.

Down Chapel Street, the Union Hotel to L, the Egyptian House to R, and St Mary's at end.

Every fortnight from 1770 there were special social gatherings, for conversation, card playing and promenade at the Ship and Castle, which was the main venue for public events. With 16 lodging rooms, five parlours, a cockfighting pit in the yard and plenty of stabling for horses and carriages, this was the natural place in 1786 for the 'elegant new theatre' to be constructed. By the following year the Theatre was open under the management of that 'Father of Provincial Drama', Richard Hughes. Later in his successful career he was to be owner/manager of the Sadlers Wells Theatre, as well as theatres in Weymouth, Plymouth, Exeter, Guernsey, Devonport, Truro and Penzance. Each theatre was open for several months of the year and Mr Hughes' company of Players moved from one theatre to the next to perform their repertoire.

The Penzance Theatre remained open until 1831, and more than 180 playbills have been traced. At its peak, in overcrowded conditions, up to 500 people could attend at one time. If resurrected, which is currently being planned, this venue might comfortably accommodate 150-200, and considerably help to restore our knowledge of the Georgian past. A Georgian Theatre Restoration Group was first set up in 1989, and currently in 2000 their lead is being reconsidered as a community project.

At the same time as the Theatre was in construction, the need for a large and commodious Assembly Room was widely expressed amongst the growing ranks of the socially minded gentry. They had the wealth, education and leisure to enjoy elegant balls, and town functions such as dinners and public receptions. A public subscription list was opened in 1786. And five years later, in 1791, the Assembly Rooms attached to the rear of the Ship and Castle Inn began their series of stated evenings for dancing, card-playing and other evening entertainments, with "never ...less than 16 or 18 couples of dancers with 3 or 4 card tables. The room very prettily lighted with 3 handsome chandeliers and 8 girandoles". (Catherine Tremenheere's diary)

Positively the last Night.

THEATRE, PENZANCE.

FOR THE BENEFIT OF

MR. J. DAWSON,

Who takes this opportunity most respectfully to announce that in consequence of the total failure of the present Theatrical Season, he has been induced (at the suggestion of many kind Friends and Patrons) to take a Benefit, and as this, in all probability, is the last time he may have occasion to intrude on the Public, in this shape, he flatters himself that Patronage will not be withheld.

In conclusion Mr. J. D. begs to say the remembrance of their manifold favors will never be effaced from his memory.

ON MONDAY, JANUARY the 10th. 1831,

Will be Performed (for the first time here) the laughable Piece of

WILLIAM THOMPSON;

Or, Which is he?

Doctor Soothem................Mr. MILLER
Mr. William Thompson, the 1st (a Gentleman subject to walk in his sleep) Mr. A. DAWSON
Bailiff, Mr. WILLIAMS | Waiter...Mr. JAMES
Mr. William Thompson, the 2nd..........Mr. J. DAWSON
Julia, Mrs. J. DAWSON | Miss Dormer, Miss J. GRANT | Mary, Miss WHITE

IN THE COURSE OF THE EVENING,

4 Comic Songs, Mr. J. Dawson,

Medley of Medleys—The Ladies—What is a Woman like ?—and Molly Pops.

A Song by Mr. Miller.

Love in Humble Life.

(By the Author of Brutus, Charles the Second, &c. &c.

Rosalara, (a Polish Sergeant) Mr. MILLER | Carlitz, Mr. J. DAWSON
Brandit, Mr. WILLIAMS
Christine....................Mrs. J. DAWSON

DEVERTISMENT OF DANCING :—

A PAS SEUL, by Miss J. DAWSON.
SAILOR's HORNPIPE by Master J. DAWSON.
Minuet di la Cour, and Gavotte, by Master and Miss J. Dawson.
COMIC DANCE by Mr. J. DAWSON.
A Sailor's Hornpipe, in Character, by Mr. J. Dawson.

The whole to conclude with the laughable Farce of

DEAF as a POST.

Mr. Simpleton........Mr. A. DAWSON | Mr. Walton........Mr. MILLER
Crupper, Master WHITE | Boots, Mr. WILLIAMS
Tristram Sappy..............................Mr. J. DAWSON
Eliza, Miss J. GRANT | Miss Walton, Miss WHITE | Mrs. Plumpley, Mrs. DAWSON
Sally Maggs..................Mrs. J. DAWSON

Doors to be open at half-past 6, to commence at 7. Half-price at half-past 8.

BOXES, 3s. PIT, 1s. 6d. GALLERY, 1s.

BOX PLACES AND TICKETS TO BE HAD OF Mr. VIGURS.

T. VIGURS, PRINTER, PENZANCE.

In 1801, in the course of changing ownership, the Ship and Castle became the Union Hotel (in celebration of the union of England and Ireland in that same year), the name by which it is known today. Its façade was rebuilt in 1825, and it remained the principal hotel in town. Quietly but surely, however, its decline as the centre of Penzance social life was speeded on by the construction of other public buildings in the town in the 19th C., and by the appearance of an even grander hotel on the promenade. The Promenade was constructed in 1844, and The Queen's Hotel in 1861. From then on the Sunday promenades were always along the 'prom'. The Union Hotel also lost its place as public assembly rooms to St. John's Hall in 1867.

Farming, Fishing and Cornish Food Riots 1709- 1859
Farming was never possible on a large scale, due to the small size of the area suitable for cultivation, the type of soil, and the fact that farmers were also part-time fishermen, millers, and sometime miners as well. In times of reasonable health when plague, pestilence, the weather or wars could be kept at bay, the farmers could raise just about enough both to survive, and to have some left over to sell at Penzance market. At other times, food was short, harvests failed, and the population grew in spurts as a new mine opened. Recruits were needed to work the mines, and Irish and Welsh migrants arrived. They required food, but were not going to help grow it, and had little time for fishing.

The 'supply and demand' principle could be seen in action, as the barter and exchange system practised in the past, had to give way to the cash economy. Farming methods continued as of old, exhausting the soil, and with little or no knowledge of improvements employed elsewhere. Cornwall as a whole, and the west in particular, was prone to angry uprisings amongst the tinners about the high price and scarcity of food.

On one occasion in 1727, miners plundered local granaries for corn, and it was only due to the generosity of Sir John St Aubyn that the crisis was overcome. Two years later an even greater rampage by miners resulted in the hanging of their leaders. Periodically over the next hundred years, skirmishes, petitions and near-riots were not uncommon.

The most common foods for families were pilchards that could be salted for keeping, other fish, bread made of barley, soups, gruels, and root vegetables, mainly potatoes. It is from the later part of the 18th C. that most cookery writers date the famous Cornish pasty, the solid and tasty food that was to feed farmers and miners alike. Generally this is agreed to have consisted of vegetables inside a dark barley corn crust, and this might be padded out with meat from small animals like rabbits. But every housewife had her favourite recipe, and far be it from this author to describe the possibilities. I would not be so bold!

From earliest times, fishing has been a mainstay of the economy of Mount's Bay. Penzance, Newlyn and Mousehole began as fishing settlements, and largely survived on their catch. Both food and employment, seasonal and fluctuating, were critical to the support of the increasing population. In 1795, a visitor described its variety:

Fishing by the Quay

"...there is a great plenty of fish, flesh and fowl. Pilchards in prodigious abundance, variety of mullets, large conger eels that weigh upwards of 70 pounds, whiting, pollock, Dories very cheap, you buy here for one shilling what would cost in London half a guinea. Large soles, halibut, plaice, flounders, lobsters, crawfish, very large crabs, very fine..." (*Through Cornwall by Coach*)

The French wars of that same period (those of the Napoleonic era), however, were soon to make inroads into that plenty. Not only was there a loss of traditional markets due to the upheavals, but also Cornish coastal trades suffered heavily, due to taxes on salt levied nationally to pay for the war effort. Salt was necessary to cure the pilchard; if it could not be got by fair means or foul, the fish would have to go to the fields as manure. Smuggling salt was a known occupation.

The Wesley Brothers, revivalism and Cornwall
In any study of Cornwall due attention must be given to John Wesley. In every town, village, hamlet or rural crossing, the traveller will find a chapel or meeting house, or four, built by his followers. The variety and quantity of these is extraordinary, and, though many have now been abandoned as places of Methodist fellowship and mission, their architectural profiles are as common as mine chimneys. It is said by some and with good reason, that John Wesley is a founding father of modern Cornwall. And that comment is not referring to buildings.

As 'first officer' in John's army of apostles and preachers, Charles Wesley, his younger brother, is known more perhaps for his hymn writing, though he too was an Anglican preacher of enormous style and persuasiveness. In his lifetime, Charles was to write more than 6,000 hymns, and no churchgoer who sings would not know them. Today, like the Welsh, the Cornish have a strong tradition of choir-singing, with the Male Voice Choirs always pulling a crowd of enthusiastic listeners.

John Wesley's Journal records his first visit to Penwith as 1743. Between that year and 1789, the Wesley brothers were to return with evangelical zeal again and again to Cornwall, with Penwith turning out to be one of their most successful mission areas. Their purposes were to revive the interest of all people in leading an enthusiastic Christian life, to re-dedicate individuals, encouraging them to be self-reliant and to improve themselves in every way. Both being Anglican priests, they nevertheless brought a passion and sentiment in their message, which appealed strongly. Halliday reminds us that:

"it must be remembered that the mining areas of the western half were then among the most densely populated parts of England, St. Just almost as big as Manchester, St. Ives considerably larger than Liverpool, and the rough and godless Celtic miners were the sort of men whom Wesley set out to save."

The population leap later was to be even more dramatic. Seventy-five mines provided employment to 16,000 people in Cornwall in 1800. Seven years later 200 mines were the place of employment to 30,000 men, women and children. This growth would serve to bring even more people into the sphere of influence we now call Methodism, even though the Wesleys had by then died.

At first it did not seem likely that west Cornwall was fertile territory for Wesley's message because of powerful opposition led locally by Dr. Walter Borlase, Vicar of Madron, a wealthy squire, and a magistrate of the Stannary Courts. Over a ten year period, by rousing worries amongst the gentry that the preacher was simply an agent for the Jacobite cause of returning a Stuart to the throne, Borlase managed to keep the missionary out of Penzance. Once the town fathers even threatened to have him jailed.

Nevertheless, John Wesley spoke everywhere possible within two miles of Penzance and elsewhere in Penwith -- St. Ives, Zennor, St. Just, Morvah, even Gulval -- and by the time of his second visit in 1744, 'Society Houses' were beginning to appear for his blessing, and for the use of his congregations. Finally, Wesley was to win through with his courage, and his willingness to speak out against the excesses and indifference of those whom the ordinary people saw as their 'rulers', governors, and sometime owners. As he grew older and more autocratic, even greater was his influence. His mission proved effective among those who had most recently lost their Cornish language, because they were the poor and least educated, as well as the ones about which the Anglican Church was least concerned. Those who resisted Wesley even though he remained an Anglican, were the most privileged, the best educated, and those who reacted strongly against the emotionalism and passion of this brand of Christianity. It was after the deaths of the brothers, and the continuation of new building for local meeting halls, Sunday schools and devotional gatherings, that moves were made to split Methodism from its Anglican revivalist roots.

The Queen's Street Methodist Chapel, which seated 1000 and was preached in by Wesley on his last joyous journey to Cornwall (1789) was officially opened the following year. A larger Wesleyan chapel in Chapel

Street, Penzance, constructed to meet the needs of an expanding congregation and seating 1350 people, was opened in 1814, and remains open and active today.

At the end of the 18th C., when both Wesleys had died, The Rev. John Skinner, another visitor on a West Country tour, made comment about Penzance and its religious practice:

"The town from this time seems to have increased both in size and population... The Chapel is dedicated to St. Mary, and furnished with a small whitewashed spire. Among the various religious sects here, may be specified, Methodists, Quakers, Presbyterians, and Jews: each having a separate place of worship."

Dipping and diving, smuggling and striving: 'fair trade'
Penzance as a town had a reputation for being prosperous, law abiding, and welcoming to visitors. Nevertheless, the Celtic nature was known to be canny, independent and sometimes foolhardy. After all, minor piracy which 'wrecking' and scavenging was, and even smuggling, is called (or was!) 'fair trading'. It was well known who the smugglers were, and not always were their judges (if they were caught and taken to court) completely clean themselves. It seemed hardly worth the bother to try and catch some of the villains if the magistrate was buying some of the goods through the back gate.

Throughout the 18th C., taxes on imported goods were ever-increasing in order to pay for ongoing national wars. To an isolated part of the country seeing little visible benefit from the government levying the tax, and in relative terms barely subsisting, it can be understood that taxation could hardly be tolerated. The differences between the continental prices and those of Britain were large, not dissimilar to the present day when 'rip-off Britain' is commonly discussed. Brandy, tobacco, salt and some 1500 items were all subject to duties, and therefore objects for smuggling. It is clear both from legend and official records, that smuggling was common, acceptable, and even well organised.

'Wrecking' (the practice of stripping ships of their cargo when wrecked on the treacherous rocks around the coast) was made a capital offence in 1753. Though it is something that has happened since ships have sailed, the long and dangerous coastline of Cornwall, plus the relative poverty and isolation of its people, allowed it to become virtually a fourth industry in the Cornish economy. There is no evidence of ships being deliberately induced onto the rocks, by the use of lights, but boats wrecked by storms could be stripped. And the general understanding was that survivors of a wreck laid claim to its salvage. Inevitably, if the wreckers were starving and the survivors were weak, the result was murderous.

The facts are always a little puzzling because wreckers were sometimes saviours of lives at the same time as they plundered the wrecks. But, certainly, some of the mobs that launched themselves onto beaches and into the sea to gather the flotsam were not only determined but desperate and vicious. The customs officers of the Penzance Custom House more than had their work cut out for them; often the mob was outside their control, and they were frightened to try and intervene.

The heyday of these lawless activities was in the second half of the 18th C. but smuggling has continued through the 19th into the 20th C. Only its nature, its practitioners and its acceptability have changed. It was more prevalent in Mousehole and Porthleven than in Penzance itself; the customs officials were thick on the ground in town, but could not be everywhere else, or get to the spot quickly enough to catch the criminals. Penzance was a sheltered haven from the south west gales, as it is today, and there were often soldiers posted in the town as well as a local Justice.

In 1846, the *Penzance Gazette* tried to explain that it was no worse here than even at the mouth of the Thames itself, but "...Whenever a wreck takes place, plunder generally ensues, be the locality where it may--and 'the people of the neighbourhood' are spoken of as 'having very improperly conducted themselves in carrying off the property,' &c., &c.; but if it happens on the coast of our County, they are at once held up to execration as 'Cornish Wreckers'." [quoted in P. Pool]

Gradually the practice died out, under the influence of the Wesleys. They were highly critical of wrecking, and it ceased due to the growing influence of their legacy in Methodism. Also the bands of volunteer militia recruited to defend Cornish coasts against invasion and privateering during the Napoleonic era, probably had their effect in terms of control over the population. Nevertheless, the legends persist, not least in more modern times, when Gilbert and Sullivan used *The Pirates of Penzance* as the tuneful reminder of our colourful past.

Penzance: A cultural exchange 'market'
The business of extracting tin and copper, and its attendant trades, was not the only market in which Penwith made exchanges. From 1801 to 1831, the population of West Cornwall doubled, but not though births alone. Coming with the influx of people were new ideas, new expectations of what was needed, and new money to help make it happen. One example that will have to stand for many others, is of friendship which brought economic rewards.

In his *History of the Cornish Copper Company*, W. H. Pascoe describes one of the major dips in the copper smelting trade when Welsh smelters forming an association amongst themselves, began to undercut Cornish smelting prices, initiating a price war. A friend in need and in deed proved to be Josiah Wedgwood, the founder of the famous pottery firm at Stoke-on-Trent. With his supporting ironmasters of Coalbrookdale, Ironbridge, that 'birthplace of the industrial revolution', they moved to bring in the financial support necessary to sustain the Cornish trade that centred upon the fine natural harbour at Hayle. Wedgwood and his family had spent several winters in the pleasant climate of Penzance, and their connections with the area were long-lasting and personal.

A son of Josiah, also called Josiah, would later invite young Thomasin

Dennis, born near Newlyn in 1770, to act as a governess and tutor to his children at their Surrey home. Her education had begun with learning to read at her mother's knee, schooling herself in the classics, and being guided in her studies by her father's friend, Davies Gilbert. The latter, living at St. Erth nearby, was to succeed the great Penzance hero, Sir Humphry Davy, as Fellow and President of the Royal Society (London).

One more example is the extraordinary and delightfully fetching Egyptian House located on Chapel across from the Union Hotel. In certainly more relaxed planning times, this relic of a mixed cultural past excites much interest in its history. Dating from about 1835, the present building replaced a dwelling house previously on the site, and was probably designed by an architect named John Foulston, who practised in Plymouth, for the purchaser John Lavin. The Penzance building resembles one he designed in Devonport, which has become the Civic and Military Library there. Lavin was to live in his building, which also housed his large collection of minerals. From his son Edward, also a mineralogist, Baroness Burdett Coutts through her agents purchased this collection and presented it to the Oxford University Museum.

The Egyptian House today, as previously in Lavin's time, offers a shop at ground level. The floors above, under the care of the Landmark Trust, are devoted to self-catering apartments for visitors. Springing from a period of popular interest in Egyptology, this building serves as an excellent reminder of Penzance's affluent and sophisticated past. By 1960 the building had become dirty and neglected, noticed by few. Through a new ownership by Norman Shipton and now that of the Landmark Trust, the wonderful building has come alive again.

Schooling Penzance
Education in the 18th and 19th centuries was developing from an informal and social class-based set of local opportunities to the formalised and governed system of today. References are made to various 'Dame Schools' (run by women who took a few pupils for learning letters),

Sunday Schools (especially after the Wesleys had come to Cornwall), the Grammar School in Penzance (first notice, 1728, for boys), the Penzance Academy, John Fennell's School (1800), the Stones' Ladies Boarding School, and one or two others. Though the Sunday Schools were free and spread around the Land's End, meant for Bible instruction as well as self-improvement, the others were generally fee-paying. Few could afford even the small amounts needed to sustain a teacher, and children were needed as additional workers in their families, whether that was fishing, farming or mining.

Often a vicar or curate might take a few pupils on a fee-paying basis, and teachers who were employed to teach in charity schools would take extra pupils singly for a small fee. A series of charity schools for teaching poor boys had been initiated by 1713, through a group of benefactors, of which John St Aubyn of the Mount was one and John Borlase of Madron another. A hundred years later, we still find education for the poor under debate. The MP for Bodmin who lived locally at St. Erth, Davies Gilbert, who himself had guided young Thomasin Dennis in her studies, nevertheless objected to instructing "the lower classes...at public expense".

In Penzance by 1812, under the leadership of the Rev. Charles Valentine Le Grice, himself a former tutor and clergyman from Norfolk who married locally, education was to be provided through the Church of England. This was education free if you could not afford it, fee-paying if you could, and supported by public subscription. From this start, the National Schools movement was to grow in Penzance and elsewhere, and with successive educational acts, to become the system we have today.

For the wealthier and primarily English speaking residents, education could be bought through the system of tutelage (taught at home) and through the time-honoured routes of the great public schools like Eton and Charterhouse, followed by Oxford or Cambridge. Specialist schools were a different matter and came into their own from about 1850 on. The first was possibly the Penzance Art School which opened in 1853 in Prince's

Street before moving to purpose-built premises in Morrab Road in 1880. In 1890 the mining classes were established in an adapted part of the Art School. Soon separate painting schools were developed also by the artists who came from all corners of the world to become 'the Newlyn School' or colony of artists.

A Newlyn School of Painting Group

The Royal Geological Society of Cornwall
In recognition of the place that the sciences held in the lives and interests of the gentlemen industrialists, medical men and mineralogists, an early learned society was formed in 1814. It proved to be the second in the country, the London Geological Society having been established seven years earlier. To it were drawn all of the local gentry of a scientific bent, including the Fox family of Falmouth, Davies Gilbert (President), Dr. John Paris, Valentine Le Grice, and even Sir Humphry Davy himself. Proceedings were published, and a distinguished library gathered. In 1867, when St. John's Hall was built, the Geological Society moved from its offices at North Parade into the west wing of the public buildings, where it remains

today. In the late 20th C. a major renovation of the west wing with a new entrance on the side, allows the visitor to view notable collections of minerals and rocks in a museum setting. Members of the Society have use of a small reference library remaining after a major auction of its documentary (mining) assets in 1999.

The School for Mining Engineers
The idea of training prospective mining men was first proposed, in 1825, by John Taylor, a land surveyor and mine manager, and one of the great pioneers of metal mining. The suggestion was taken up by the MP, Sir Charles Lemon, and an experimental school was set up in Truro in 1839 with no success, tried again in 1840 and failed again. In 1853, another attempt was made at the Royal Institution of Cornwall in Truro, which limped along for six years before closing. Meanwhile the Miners' Association and the Royal School of Mines had been founded and was spreading through papers delivered in church halls and elsewhere by men of practical experience to 'untaught miners' in their (all too little) spare time.

The classes were held from St. Just in the west to Tavistock in the east, and three full-time mining schools, called the science schools, were established at Camborne, Redruth and Penzance (in the Art School Building on Morrab Road). In 1883, on a site near Camborne provided by G.L. Basset, a special building for classrooms, offices as well as laboratories, was opened. In stages until 1895 the whole of the Camborne School of Mines was developed. In 1909, the individual schools were amalgamated and located in their present location, under the title of the School of Metalliferous Mining (Cornwall) at Camborne. The Redruth and Penzance schools continued to provide evening science courses and art classes thereafter and became part of the general provision of adult education.

Two men and a woman from West Cornwall:
Humphry Davy, Maria Branwell, William Lovett

Sir Humphry Davy

Continuing the theme of Penzance as a place that opened its doors more widely in the 18th and 19th centuries, welcoming visitors of many types and purposes, there are those who made a lasting mark elsewhere. Throughout the ups and downs of the gradual decline of industrial Cornwall, thousands moved to other countries -- Australia, South Africa, the Americas -- with their understanding and experience of hard-rock in the mines of Cornwall. Whole books are written on the impact of the Cornish miner abroad. Now at the beginning of the third millennium Cornwall is feeling an upsurge of interest from these Cornish Connections who flood the county again looking for their roots.

Sir Humphry Davy

By the time Humphry Davy was born in a house on the Terrace of Market Jew Street in 1778, Penzance was already the social and educational centre of West Cornwall. From 1770 there had been a Ladies' Book Club and circulating library, soon followed by a Gentlemen's Book Club, from which young Davy would borrow. His wider family spread over Penwith from Gulval to St. Just, and included such as the Borlase family of Pendeen, and, most importantly, the Tonkin family of Penzance. Dr. John Tonkin, his guardian and godfather, an apothecary to whom young Davy would first apprentice himself, was the most important influence in his life, though his love and care for his mother and for his Penzance home were always there.

The story of Davy's brilliant life, his successes in the scientific world of British and European achievement, and yet his life-long concern and love for Cornwall, cannot be told here in any detail. At home in Penzance, during his life-time and with his interest, both the Royal Geological Society of Cornwall (1807) and the Morrab Library (1818, until the late 20th C. called The Penzance Library) were both established. Davy's story is one in its own right and told not only by his brother, Dr. John Davy, who wrote his biography after Humphry's early death in 1829, but more recently and with great elegance by the late Cornish author, Anne Treneer. This reference is included in the reading trail.

Maria Branwell Bronte

When baby Davy was being baptised at St. Mary's Chapel, a few doors up Chapel Street Thomas Branwell and his wife Anne Carne were bringing their own large family into the world. Only four daughters and one son survived infancy of the eleven who were born, and those brought up at No. 25 Chapel Street were Elizabeth, Maria, Jane and Charlotte Branwell and their brother Benjamin (Mayor of Penzance, 1809-10). Aunt Jane Branwell, their father's sister, was a great favourite of the children's, and she married the schoolmaster, John Fennell, who wrote for Methodist magazines and organised Wesleyan activities at the new Methodist Chapel up the street.

The Fennells left Penzance to live in Yorkshire where John was to become Head Master of a Methodist school, and, in 1812, at the age of 29, Maria went from Penzance by stage coach to visit her relatives at their school near Leeds. There she was to fall in love at first sight with the Rev. Patrick Bronte. In the nine years of their marriage, they produced three daughters, Charlotte, Emily, and Anne and one son, Branwell. Those three daughters, despite their mother's illness and death by the time of their teens, were steeped in knowledge of Penzance.

Where their mother Maria left off in tales of her childhood, her sister Elizabeth, ('Aunt Branwell' to the children) stepped in as substitute and storyteller. Today we know of Charlotte, Emily and Anne Bronte as three of Britain's greatest creative writers. Anne in her novel, *The Tenant of Wildfell Hall*, makes one of her fictional characters casually mention the latest and last book of Sir Humphry Davy, *Consolations in Travel, or Last Days of a Philosopher.*

A miniature drawing of Maria Branwell

William Lovett

Born in 1800, in very different circumstances at nearby Newlyn, was another remarkable man, William Lovett. The son of a mariner who died before he was born, William was brought up amongst the poorest of the working class by his mother, Keziah Green. Her precarious living as a fish jouster (seller) -- one who walked from house to house with a basket of fish on her back --meant that young Lovett was apprenticed first to a ropemaker.

Industrial changes meant that chains replaced ropes, and at the age of 21 he left Cornwall forever to become first a cabinetmaker, then a sweet shop owner with his wife, a lady's maid. During his long life he studied busily on a wide range of subjects. When that shop failed as did a coffee house soon after, he and his wife became deeply involved in the co-operative movement and in various political and reform issues.

Perhaps Lovett's most important contribution to the life of the nation was during the 1830s when he drafted the main points of the 'People's Charter' which included major reforms like universal suffrage (to include women as voters), and thereby became 'the greatest radical secretary of the working class'. For one year beginning in 1939, he was imprisoned at Warwick Gaol for the state crime of seditious libel, and his incarceration under terrible conditions, broke his health. Nevertheless, in the 1840s he was active in the Anti-Slavery League. Throughout his long and quite hard life he was honest, sincere and courageous, and a friend to progress. He died in 1877 and his boyhood home in Newlyn was on the site of the Centenary Chapel. A plaque to his memory hangs on the Smugglers' Hotel, and was re-gilded in 1977, cost covered by collection at a celebratory talk about Lovett by Michael Foot.

Come the Railway, come the artists, come the....
Peter Pool in his full *History of Penzance*, describes well what a man born in 1800 and living to a normal old age of 70 or more, would have seen within the span of his 19th C. life:

"...[he] would have known in his youth a town essentially similar to that which received the Charter in 1614, and lived to spend his last years in one as similar to that which we know today. He would have seen the erection of the new St. Mary's Chapel and its change of status years later to that of a Church; the entry of the first steamship into the harbour in 1825, and successive enlargements of the harbour itself to its present form; the building of the new Market House in 1838 and of the Public Buildings [Ref: St. John's Hall and the courts] in 1867, the erection of the statue of Sir Humphry Davy in 1872 (paid for by subscription of the working men of the town); the coming of the railway and the consequent revolution in communications with the outside world; the building of the promenade in 1844 and its connection with Alverton by Alexandra Road (1865) and Morrab Road (1881); the tripling of the population of the town from 3,382 in 1801 to 10,425 in 1871; and growth of the built-up area to fill almost all available space within the borough boundary."

That very long sentence sums up a span of time in which change speeded up at a rate never seen before in Penzance. And, certainly the most significant of the topics mentioned is the coming of the railway in 1852 to the Mount's Bay area. Prior to that date three mineral railways had operated in Cornwall connecting tin and copper mines with their ports and harbours, but these had not challenged the fairly isolated community life that was still possible in West Cornwall.

A two-stage process carried forward by the West Cornwall Railway, allowed for the Redruth to Penzance section to open in 1852, and the extension from Redruth to Truro in 1855. It was not until 1859, as Isambard Kingdom Brunel (1806-59) was dying, that his marvellous Royal Albert Bridge over the Tamar, opened the through line for the use of passengers from Penzance to Plymouth and on to Paddington. It is of more than passing interest to realise that at the same time as Brunel was acting as Chief Engineer to the Great Western Railway, he was also designing hospital buildings for the use of Florence Nightingale and her nurses in the Crimea.

Because a change of trains was necessary at Truro, due to a different size of gauge in the west from that in the east, the quickest journey between Penzance and Paddington was 11 hours and 50 minutes. After 1877, with adjusted rails, changing at Truro was abolished and this cut the time of the fastest train to eight hours and 55 minutes.

Going out of Cornwall
The benefits of the railway to West Cornwall were immense, and mainly because of sales that could be made of fresh produce, fish, broccoli, potatoes, other vegetables, and for the first time, flowers. Because of the climate it was possible for farmers to turn to market gardening, and this would include produce from the Isles of Scilly. The fisheries, too, received a new lease of life. Though pilchards were still cured, packed in barrels and sent off to Italy (as they are today), other fresh fish such as mackerel had previously been sold only around the port for home consumption. Now they could be delivered to London within the day. A tremendous rush of boat-building began and by 1875, there were some 400 fishing boats in Mount's Bay. During the season the fishermen landed some 50 tons of fish a day.

By the end of the 19th C., however, the death knell for both the mines and the fisheries had been sounded. It is again with Halliday, that we find the apt summary of the railway as a two-edged sword:
"Then, the railway that had brought prosperity to the mackerel fisheries of Mount's Bay, St. Ives and Mevagissey was to prove by no means an unmixed blessing. For many years trawlers from Plymouth and Brixham had been visiting western waters, dragging their trawls over the bottom of the fishing grounds by day, and carrying their catches back by night in order to reach the nearest big market at Plymouth. As the Cornish drifters fished by night this did not greatly matter, but with the opening of the Cornwall Railway foreign trawlers could fish day and night and send off their catches from Penzance like the local men...easy access to eastern markets attracted boats from farther afield, from Yarmouth and Lowestoft, their trawls fouling and cutting the local drift nets. Moreover, the foreigners fished on Sundays, a practice so abhorrent...to the Mount's Bay Methodists that at last they could bear it no longer...one morning in 1896 they attacked their rivals...It was a final gesture of despair."

In the spring of 1896, the Newlyn fisherman finally decided they had put up long enough with the landing of Sunday catches by foreigners, the so-called 'Yorkies' (Lowestoft fleets). Artists, too, had complained rather bitterly, that their landladies would not allow them to paint in their rooms on Sundays. But the fishermen, had let their Sundays stretch out to the weekend and Fridays as well. If others were going to persist in landing fish seven days a week, their own livelihoods were put at risk.

About a thousand men and women from Newlyn participated in the skirmishes, and also sent for help from nearby harbours. Their objective was to board the offending boats (up to about 50) and throw their catches away...some hundred thousand mackerel were returned to the sea from 15 or 16 boats before much could be done.

Porthleven fishermen arrived to help their friends on the second day, by which time a contingent of police from all over west Cornwall and as far as Camborne, had converged upon Newlyn. It became a battle between on the one side Newlyn, Porthleven and St. Ives fishermen, and on the other the Lowestoft and Penzance people, police, and by now the military. It was the soldiers who were finally to finish it. The 'Riot Act' had been threatened but not read out. In 1999, the Cornish-born playwright and actor, Nick Darke, was to turn this locally famous event into a rather farcical comedy, performed by the Cornish theatrical company Kneehigh in London and Cornwall, calling it simply *The Riot*.

Though nothing to do with the railway, mining was also reaching its end. As the easily accessible deposits were exhausted, deeper mining costing more, the price of tin began to fall. Other sources were coming onto to the world market, places as far afield as Malaya and the United States could provide what was needed at a cheaper price. One after another of the mines in West Cornwall closed. "The old Cornish [drinking] toast of 'Fish, Tin and Copper' had become tragically ironical; a more relevant one would have been 'China Clay and Tourists'.

Coming into Cornwall
It was, of course, the trains that brought the tourists, but rather more importantly it brought new settlers of a kind not familiar to west Cornwall. The story of the coming of the artists -- Walter Langley, Stanhope Forbes,

OPENING OF THE WEST CORNWALL RAILWAY.—THE PENZANCE STATION.

The Railway Terminus, Penzance

Frank Bramley, Elizabeth Armstrong, Lamorna Birch, Laura Knight-- is now so widely told and so well documented that to try and summarise the influx of the species, both to the north coast (St Ives and around) and the south coast (Newlyn and around) is nigh impossible in a few sentences. But, the immigration cannot be neglected, if an accurate history of Penzance and area, its assets and resources, is to be understood and harnessed for the future.

The paintings, sculptures, and crafts of the Newlyn artists and those who were to follow after them, have left a treasure as important and interesting as an archaeological site. Delving into the history of an art object, its maker, and the environment in which it was produced, is also a mining project though obviously of a different kind. The search for accurate information could even be described as 'a fishing trip' not least because there is an ocean of material out there, both visual and academic, fact and theory. The only traditional industry that perhaps art cannot be likened to is farming, and not only because the product is not edible, but because of its individual nature as created by one artist.

Stemming from the sometime migration of artists to make West Cornwall their creative base (even if maintaining a flat in London), a plea went up for an art gallery in the 1890s. Church halls and private studios had been used for exhibitions around Newlyn, as artists worked from home even though they painted on the street corners and at the quays. But, the need was for an exhibition space in a central location where visitors could be welcomed at all times, and where artists could hang their latest work before perhaps sending it to major exhibition centres for showing and selling. John Passmore Edwards, a wealthy and philanthropic Cornishman heard the plea and offered to Stanhope Forbes and his colleagues, a gallery of their own. Charles Le Grice offered a plot of land on Newlyn Green, and there Passmore Edwards paid for the Newlyn Art Gallery to be constructed, dedicated as it is to John Opie, then Cornwall's most famous artist son. From 1895 to the present day, stopping only briefly during the First World War, a continuous show of art has been available to all comers, be they local or just visiting.

THE PASSMORE EDWARDS ART GALLERY NEWLYN CORNWALL. JAS HICKS ARCHT

Legend and literature

Humphry Davy (1778-1829)

Perhaps the most important writer to emerge from Penzance was Humphry Davy, best known now for the invention of the miner's safety lamp. Becoming both a professor of chemistry and President of the Royal Institution in London, he moved in the highest intellectual circles of Britain and Europe. His friends numbered many of the leading writers of the day, Samuel Taylor Coleridge, William Wordsworth, Sir Walter Scott (a relation of his wife) and numerous others, but he decided upon a scientific career rather than a literary one. Nevertheless, he never completely stopped writing poetry. A statue of him is found at the top of Market Jew Street in Penzance in front of the Market House.

Best seen as a Cornish romantic poet, Davy repeatedly turns to the natural world around Penzance, finding there a truth and value lost by most rational writers. This emphasis on what is natural and uncorrupted leads to an emphasis on the importance of the emotions and the feelings. Among the poems inspired by his childhood in the Mount's Bay area are 'In Ludgvan Churchyard', 'The Sons of Genius', 'The Tempest' and 'Ode to Saint Michael's Mount'. Perhaps his greatest poem, however, is 'Mount's Bay' that somehow captures an ancient view of the ocean.

On the sea
The sunbeams tremble; and the purple light
Illumes the dark Bolerium, seat of storms.
High are his granite rocks. His frowning brow
Hangs o'er the smiling Ocean. In his caves,
Th'Atlantic breezes murmur. In his caves,
Where sleep the haggard Spirits of the storm,
Wild dreary are the schistine rocks around
Encircled by the wave, where to the breeze
The haggard Cormorant shrieks. And far beyond
Are seen the cloud-like Islands, grey in mists.

Years ago, there was a marsh between Penzance and Newlyn, known to the old people as the "Clodgy". When the sea moaned there, they said, "Clodgy is calling for rain." Sometimes in the late 19 C. it was "Bucca is calling". 'Bucca' is the Cornish word for a ghost or spirit, and also the nickname in Penzance for the inhabitants of Newlyn:

> Penzance boys up in a tree,
> Looking as wisht as wisht can be;
> Newlyn 'Buccas', strong as oak,
> Knocking them down at every poke.

Thomas Hardy (1840-1928)

In 1870, Thomas Hardy, a young architectural assistant came to north Cornwall from his native Dorset. Aside from meeting his wife-to-be in this magic land, in one way and another he was also to employ the foremost legends of the Cornish in his future writings as poet and novelist. His major fictional construction was his vision of his native Dorset as the legendary kingdom of Wessex; the Outer-Wessex included Cornwall, an area he was to call 'Lyonnesse'.

The only one of his stories to be placed in Penzance, which he re-names Pen-zephyr, is 'A Mere Interlude' (1885). It is the story of a young schoolteacher named Baptista Trewthen, returning home to Scilly to marry an older Scillonian man named David Heddegan. She finds herself drawn to an old flame called Charles Stow on the streets of Pen-zephyr while waiting for her sailing, and elects to marry him instead. He immediately drowns in Mount's Bay and remarriage to Heddegan is her only solution. Read the story for what happens next.

Elizabeth Catherine Thomas Carne (1817-1873)

Elizabeth Carne was the daughter of the eminent geologist, Joseph Carne (1782-1850), a partner in the Penzance Bank, an Alderman and Justice of the Peace for Penzance. At the age of 15, she was noticed in his diary as 'a remarkable person', by the philosopher and historian John Stuart Mill. Mill, a friend of her father's on his first walking tour of Land's End in 1832, was much impressed with Elizabeth's intelligence and curiosity. Later, he was to meet and become friends with the famous Quaker family of Falmouth, the Foxes, and was not at all surprised to learn of the close friendship between the two literary women, Elizabeth Carne and Caroline Fox.

Though never to achieve the fame of the diarist Caroline Fox, Elizabeth was also an exceptional literary woman. Her writings included papers on the metamorphosis of rocks in the Land's End district, and also on similar topics in the Alpine regions of Europe where she travelled. After her father's death, she used his money for the benefaction of Penzance by funding schools, and also the original geological museum to house her collection. Aside from her scientific interests, until her death in 1873, she was head of the Penzance Bank of Batten Carne & Carne.

Mrs. Craik (Dinah Maria Mulock) (1826-1887)
In 1882, the most prolific novelist, essayist, translator and poet of the Victorian literary scene toured in Cornwall, bringing with her two nieces -- a first visit for them all. Mrs. Craik was the famous author of *John Halifax, Gentleman*, a bestseller of its day, and a book that was reprinted so many times, that its copies exist in millions. Her fictional hero, John Halifax, upon which she was to build her long literary career, was a Cornish lad, an orphan of the working class, who rose to become a gentleman. A study of her vast bibliography shows that she often mentions Cornwall in her novels, sometimes in depth when telling about the distressing closure of the mines. So we can believe her in Chapter One of *An Unsentimental Journey Through Cornwall*, where she writes:
"I had always wished to investigate Cornwall. This desire had existed ever since, at five years old, I made acquaintance with Jack the Giantkiller, and afterwards, at fifteen or so, fell in love with my life's one hero, King Arthur.
"Between these two illustrious Cornishmen, --equally mythical, practical folk would say -- there exists more similarity than at first appears. The aim of both was to uphold right and to redress wrong. Patience, self-denial, tenderness to the weak and helpless, dauntless courage against the wicked and the strong: these, the essential elements of true manliness, characterise both the humble Jack and the kingly Arthur. And the qualities seem to have "Art

descended to more modern times...I wanted to see if the same spirit lingered yet, as I had heard it did among Cornish folk, which, it was said, were a race by themselves, honest, simple, shrewd, and kind. Also I wished to see the Cornish land and especially the Land's End."

She could not advise Marazion as a bathing place -- 'a small ugly fishy-smelling beach' but St. Michael's Mount was beyond compare: "oh! what a beautiful spot it is!...Such a curious mingling of a mediaeval fortress and modern residence; of antiquarian treasures and everyday business; for at the foot of the rock is a fishing village of about thirty cottages which carries on a thriving trade; ...How in the world do the St Aubyns manage when they go out to dinner?"
Penzance for Mrs. Craik was "...pretty but so terribly 'genteel,' so extremely civilised...But the neighbourhood of Penzance is lovely. Shrubs and flowers such as one sees on the shores of the Mediterranean..."

The town of Penzance also features heavily in such novels as R.M. Ballantyne's *Deep Down: A Tale of Cornish Mines* (1868) and Walter Besant's *Armorel of Lyonesse: A Romance of Today* (1890). For a tale of wreckers, no better can be found that James F. Cobb's *The Watchers on the Longships.* (1878).

Reading trail for Chapter 3

Louise Courtney (1878) *Half a Century of Penzance, 1825-1875* (from notes by J.S. Courtney), Penzance: Beare & Son. Reprinted by P. Dalwood, 1972 and Oakmagic Publications, 1999.

Margaret A. Courtney (1890) *Folklore and Legends of Cornwall [Cornish Feasts and Folklore]* reprinted Exeter: Cornwall Books, 1989.

Mrs. Craik (1884) *An Unsentimental Journey through Cornwall,* London: Macmillan. Reprinted by Jamieson Library, Newmill, Penzance, 1988.

Melissa Hardie, Editor (1992) *A Mere Interlude: Some Literary Visitors to Lyonnesse,* Penzance: The Patten Press.

Kerrow Hill (1994) *The Bronte Sisters and Sir Humphry Davy, A sharing of visions,* Newmill: The Jamieson Library.

Vida Heard (1984) *Cornish Cookery, Recipes of Today and Yesteryear,* Redruth: Dyllansow Truran.

W. H. Hudson (1908), *The Land's End.* Reprinted London: Wildwood 1981.

Marazion History Group (1995) *The Charter Town of Marazion,* Marazion Town Trust.

W. H. Pascoe (n.d., about 1983) *C.C.C. The History of the Cornish Copper Company,* Redruth: Dyllansow Truran.

John Pearce (1964) *The Wesleys in Cornwall,* Truro: D. Bradford Barton Ltd.

Penwith Local History Group (2000) *In and around Penzance during Napoleonic Times,* Penzance.

K. R. Pieterse (n.d.) *Early Moves to Train Mining Engineers in Cornwall Leading to the Foundation of the School of Mines.*

Edgar A. Rees (1956) *Old Penzance,* Penzance: The author.

Anne Treneer (1963) *The Mercurial Chemist: Humphry Davy,* London: Methuen & Co.

John Vivian (n.d.) *Tales of the Cornish Wreckers,* Truro: Tor Mark Press.

John Watney (1998) *The Industrial Revolution,* Andover: Pitkin Guides.

CHAPTER 4

THE TWENTIETH CENTURY
A CHANGED AND CHANGING PLACE

"Art and colonisation do not always accompany each other, but they are, all the same, two distinguishing elements of human activity; and it so happens that whilst artists are forming a colony of their own in Cornwall, Cornishmen, in greater proportion to the inhabitants of any English portion to the inhabitants of any English county, are peopling the new colonies of the world. One of my motives in complying with the request made to me to build an Art Gallery in Newlyn was to assist to root these artistic colonists in that locality. Being there, I should like to keep them there!

I am, naturally, interested in anything appertaining to the good of Cornwall; and as the mines of Cornwall are drying up, under the soil, I am desirous that the world at large should know more of the scenic wealth of Cornwall on the soil, and which was scattered in rich abundance around its rugged rock-bound coasts. The Newlyn School and Colony of Artists are illustrating and interpreting that wealth in line and colour on canvas and thereby benefiting themselves, Cornwall and the world."

John Passmore Edwards

On the laying of the memorial stone of the Newlyn Art Gallery, 1895

In giving this further gift to his native land, one amongst the many he presented to Cornwall, Passmore Edwards admitted to the reality of changing fortunes. More importantly, he pointed to solutions with his own life experiences to prove his case. In our day we call it "putting his money where his mouth is" and Passmore Edwards certainly did that again and again.

The leading men at the time, those who attended the opening luncheon to celebrate the new Gallery, held at the Queen's Hotel, October 22, 1895, were all in good form. They laughed and cheered as speaker after speaker shed new light on the theme of arts and community, and how the new institution might support itself. The gentlemen who spoke were optimistic and humorous: The Right Hon. Lord St. Levan, Leonard H. Courtney, M.P. and T.B. Bolitho, M.P., Arthur Quiller-Couch, the novelist, a churchman, three Justices of the Peace, and one doctor, and their wives were in attendance. In the evening a 'conversazione' was held in the Gallery itself, with music and dramatic sketches &c. at which some gentlemen and ladies assisted. Here was a triumph! A jewel in the crown for Mount's Bay, but nevertheless one that the working world of Newlyn would seldom notice...

It was not five years before, in hindsight, that Penzance had reached its zenith, its 'summit of prosperity', according to Peter Pool in his *History of Penzance.*

"Everything for which generations of townsmen had worked seemed to have been achieved; a large harbour, swift communications with the outside world, splendid public buildings...the whole history of the borough and town seems a story of steady growth to the position attained in the late 19th C; the growth then stopped and an almost imperceptible decline began; Penzance had achieved what it had sought only to find that, somehow, it was no longer enough."

The decline to which Pool refers was that of the economic underpin of the area, not just the town itself. It was still a port, still a market town, still a centre for culture, but no longer was the money in circulation that was generated by the mining industry. Pool describes these mines as seeming to be "features of the Penwith scene as permanent as the quoits and church towers". But, of course, it was not that the mine chimneys disappeared, but that they closed for business. Between 1852 and 1913, Cornwall produced 99% of Britain's overall production of tin. Cornish mines had also accounted for 50% of Britain's non-ferrous metal production.

By also referring to the world-wide diaspora of the Cornish seeking work in foreign parts, Passmore Edwards was recognising the population decline which operated throughout this period, and we may say, to some extent, to this day. In the final 40 years of the 20th C., Cornwall had lost 50,000 of its population through emigration, and the worst of it was that these were some of the most vigorous, working people whose leaving also showed initiative and drive.

Passmore Edwards, a successful London newspaperman by trade, well knew that the mines of the area were closing: Balleswidden (1873), Ding Dong (1878), Wheal Owles (1893) and Botallack (1895), and that there was an attending slide for the smelting works. Even the great smelting works at Chyandour, the largest in Cornwall was to close in 1912. But, before he would report that closure as one more nail in the coffin of the mining industry (there would be more), Passmore Edwards, also known as 'Mr Greatheart' and the 'Cornish Carnegie' himself was dead.

From *The West Briton*, April 27, 1911

" ...There are few Cornish lads who have attained a more eminent position as reformer and philanthropist than Mr. Passmore Edwards. He was born on March 24, 1823 at Blackwater, his father being a carpenter. The only education he had was at the village school, his teacher being a former miner. He read all the books he could get hold of, often walking to Truro to buy a book for which he had saved his pence. It was by the dim light of a single candle that this illustrious gentleman managed to pick up fragments of knowledge, and it was the recollection of this early struggle that encouraged him in later years to promote the public library movement, so that poor boys and girls, besides men and women, might enjoy the educational advantages denied to them during the early and middle parts of last century. His first start was made as Manchester correspondent of a London paper at a salary of £40 a year. After remaining in Manchester about five years he tried his fortune in London, where he obtained a firm footing as a journalist. From 1874 to 1880 he sat in Parliament for Salisbury in the Liberal interest.

What the subsequent newspaper listing of sixteen institutions given to Cornwall through Passmore Edwards' generosity -- primarily libraries, schools and hospitals -- tells us about Penzance is quite a lot, and should be appreciated. Penzance already had its libraries and literary societies and still does. Penzance had its long tradition of dispensary and medical care: in 1809 the Penzance Public Dispensary and Humane Society was founded; in 1874 the Infirmary at St. Clare was established. Penzance already had its mining and science schools. In fact, as Daniel Defoe reported in 1724, Penzance was a "well set up town". What Penzance had now was a cluster, a group, a 'colony' of creative and artistic people who had gathered in the area, for the quality of light, the quality of independence and rurality, and not least the quality of the friendships they would make.

From *The Cornishman*, August 1995

"...the self-styled colony of artists settled in Newlyn...consciously seeking a place where they could pursue the kind of lifestyle and painting they had encountered in Continental art colonies such as Pont Aven in Brittany. They had adopted the practice -- at that time considered revolutionary -- of painting in the open air, and they lived -- as they believed -- in close contact with the local fishing and farming community, whose lives and surroundings formed the subjects of their works...The opening of the Gallery in 1895 embodied this sense of belonging: it was, said Stanhope Forbes, meant to serve the locality, as a "public institution, not an artists' club".

The artists were not always to be believed, especially in earlier days when the Gallery was more of a 'gentlemen's club'. But, a contemporary public institution is what Passmore Edwards intended to give, and what the Art Gallery at the end of the 20th C. has become for the western end of Cornwall. The words of a Newlyn boy, a bona-fide Bucca, are to be read and digested:

"[The Newlyn Art Gallery is]...A special place for me -- apart from the chapel and school I attended -- for some time, it was the biggest building I had ever seen. Yet it was to be in situ for half a century and more before I crossed its threshold. After all, one had to pay to go in there and in those "Hungry Thirties" pennies were precious...sometime in the late 1940s...I wanted to know what all the fuss was about. I had no idea that my appetite for sensation would lead to such a long association with the Art Gallery, a period of more years than I care to count spent writing about its exhibitions and events. If nothing else, this period has brought home to me that it is the people passing through its portals, not as long-lived as its granite and slate, that have made, are making and will make the art gallery the place it is." [Frank Ruhrmund, Arts Editor, *The Cornishman*]

The whole person, and healthy too
In 1907, the 75th Annual Meeting of the British Medical Association was held at Exeter, and for this occasion a very grand guide-book was produced for the delegates, called *A Book of The South West*. The purpose was to provide "a reliable work of reference for those [doctors] who may be called upon to recommend a locality in Devonshire or Cornwall, either for a short stay or for permanent residence." This was a time, of course, before antibiotics, when climate was an important element in cure (or believed to be) and convalescence often meant at least a short period of migration to a balmier place. Amongst places of healthy resort is:
"Penzance, Population 13,136
130 miles from Exeter, the terminus of the GWR [The Great Western or 'God's Wonderful Railway']

Penzance is a fast-growing resort, renowned for its mild climate and interesting surroundings. It is one of the most enterprising Cornish towns, and offers organised pleasures to the visitor...The public buildings, a generation old, form a fine group, and contain the Guildhall, Public Library, a good Geological Museum, and St. John's Hall, where good concerts and lectures are held...The Morrab Gardens are a living witness to the mildness of the climate: here palms, cacti, camelias, aloes and olives luxuriate in prodigal profusion...these results are due to the absence of cold rather than to a great heat...The natural beauties have caused the well-known school of Newlyn artists to found a permanent colony. The town itself has but little of interest outside the features mentioned!"

Apart from an improvement in the general health and hygiene of the population, brought forward by the organisation and provision of health and environmental services in the United Kingdom as a whole, Cornwall's advances in the 20th C. have been dramatic. The provision of clean water, improved sewerage, public housing and the closure of the mines are largely responsible.

In the 19th C. amongst 206 male workers of the average age of 26 at Ding Dong Mine, in Madron, more than a quarter were under 15 years, two being 8 years old. Dr. Richard Quiller Couch who carried out the health survey on mining workers in 1857, estimated that half the deaths of the mining population were due to chest complaints and an average length of life was 47 years. As a kind of yardstick of health improvements in the 20th C., statistics for the whole of Cornwall in the 19th C. show that 65% of all males and 46% of all females died before the age of 5 years.

Women packing pilchards, Newlyn

Votes for Women

Harking back to Celtic times, there has always been an unusual, though one could equally say, unacknowledged, respect and regard for women within the Cornish community. The reader will recall the lady, Alice de Lisle, from Chapter 1, Maria Branwell from Chapter 2, Elizabeth Carne from Chapter

3. These were not, of course, the only women to have taken a decisive role in their community or family life, nor even if a popular poll were to be taken, would they be recognised at all. But popular fame does not necessarily, if ever, reflect economic and social importance to the life of a town or a village. How these survive, and move forward, is just as often down to the women as to men, perhaps more.

The latter part of the 19th C. and the whole of the 20th C. were times when recognition of the varied roles undertaken by women, an acceptance of more like an equal political partnership between men and women, was demanded. This campaign for social and economic justice as well as political equality was, of course, both national and international in its drive, and sometimes violent and confrontational in its presentation. But, the impulses were the same as those that pushed anti-slavery reforms, William Lovett of Newlyn and the Chartists, Education Acts, John Stuart Mill and his political writings, Bertrand and Dora Russell in their 'New Age' ideas for change. All of these had Cornish connection with Penwith.

Some saw no purpose in extending the vote to women, because after all, their vote could be expressed through their men. But others disagreed, upheld the principle if not always the fact, of equal representation, and the World Wars ahead would serve also to underline the importance of women pulling their political weight in civic affairs. Several people in the Penzance area are known to have worked toward the enfranchisement of women through public meetings, and petitions. No damage to property or person, nor even 'ugly moments' occurred in Cornwall, and this may partly be due to a long Celtic tradition of egalitarianism. Notably those who supported the campaign in Penwith were:

Leonard Courtney, later Lord Courtney of Penwith
Rev. Prebendary Philip Hedgeland, Vicar of St. Mary's Church and Archivist of the Morrab Library Mrs. Robins Bolitho (Augusta Jane Wilson, native of Yorkshire) of Trengwainton, who in 1920 became Cornwall's first woman magistrate
Mrs. J.B. Cornish (Margaret Hadow, native of Gloucestershire), niece of Archdeacon Cornish, Vicar of Kenwyn and later Bishop of St. Germans, who married her cousin John, the Penzance solicitor and Treasurer of the Newlyn Art Gallery for 30 years.

Mrs. Moffat Lindner (Augusta Smith), daughter of the Royal Academy painter, F.M. Smith, and a painter in her own right, who came to St. Ives to learn to paint with Julius Olssen, then married a fellow painter. On the list of signatories to the first petition, was the Canadian artist, Elizabeth Armstrong Forbes, who in 1889 had married the premier member of the Newlyn School of painters, Stanhope Forbes. She had died of cancer (1912) before women in Britain received the vote.

In 1918, partial enfranchisement was granted to women over the age of 30, and in 1928 universal suffrage was achieved on an equal basis. Cornwall and Penzance did its bit.

It is of interest to note that all of the above were in attendance at the opening ceremonies of the Newlyn Art Gallery with the exception of the Lindners who are of the next generation and may not have arrived in Cornwall by 1895. But, Leonard Courtney, received the greatest billing and was the main speaker for the Newlyn occasion.

Leonard Courtney, MP, (1832-1918)
Courtney should be Penzance's second favourite son, if Humphry Davy can be said to be first. Not mentioned at all in Pool's history, he seems to have faded from popular memory. But in his day, his importance was a match for Davy's as earlier it would have been a match for Godolphin's.

Leonard Courtney was the eldest son of John and Sarah Courtney of Alverton House in Penzance, and worked as a boy in Bolitho's Bank (now Barclays Bank PLC on Market Jew Street). His mathematical talents were recognised and a scholarship to Cambridge preceded his call to the bar at Lincoln's Inn, London. As a leader-writer at *The Times*, he produced some 3,000 articles in 16 years, while also contributing to the *Fortnightly Review*. From 1872 to 1875 he held the Chair of Political Economy at University College, London, and entered Parliament as a Liberal in 1875.

In 1878 he became leader of the pro-suffrage MPs, was a friend of the President of the National Union of Women's Suffrage Societies, Millicent Garrett Fawcett, and continued to support the cause until his death. His wife, Catherine Potter, was the daughter of the some time Chairman of the Great Western Railway, and the sister of the social reformer and intellectual, Beatrice Webb. The latter with her husband, Sydney, founded the London School of Economics.

As a person, he was known for "opposing everywhere the spirit of domination" and was an ardent supporter of proportional representation as a means of protecting minorities. Successively he became under-secretary for the Home Office, then under-secretary for the Colonies, and in 1882, secretary of the Treasury, which promised Cabinet office. But that was not to be, due to falling out with Gladstone by opposing Home Rule for Ireland. Pressed to become the Speaker of the House of Commons, he refused in order to preserve his political freedom, a typical step for Courtney.

In the *Dictionary of National Biography*, Courtney is described as "... perhaps the greatest British statesman, since Cobden, of those who have never held Cabinet office. He was a genial host, fond of society, in argument dogmatic and sometimes pragmatical, stiff in opinions, and always ready to sacrifice his career to his convictions. To a mathematical mind and a strong logical sense, which insisted on arguing out every question, he united a very warm and emotional disposition." To this writer, that sounds like a 'true Cornishman'. And one we should always remember.

The World Wars
The West Country writer, Sheila Bird, aside from providing us with some previously unpublished photographs of *Bygone Penzance and Newlyn*, relates in vivid form the themes and activities introduced by the declaration of 'Europe at War' on 6 August 1914.

"There was a flurry of local activity as more reservists were called up, and there was a big recruitment drive. German aliens were taken into custody at Chyandour and searched for weapons, but none were found...The railway station became the scene of many stirring, stiff-upper-lip, patriotic departures with military music and hearty cheers. The port of Penzance became an auxiliary naval base and Holman's offices were used as the regional headquarters for naval personnel...Women and girls were put to agricultural work. Hampers of vegetables were sent to sailors and weekly consignments of eggs were dispatched to the National Egg Collection...Girl Guides collected silver paper and waste paper to boost the war effort and a number of war relief funds were set up..."

Standing on the headland, near the site of the early St. Anthony's Chapel, is the War Memorial erected to honour those who died from Penzance in the 'Great War'. Similar monuments are to be found in surrounding towns and villages. Little did anyone imagine who celebrated with dances and processions and ship sirens in 1918, that within another generation, another great war, World War II, would be faced. In the year 2000, a major photographic exhibition is to be held at Penlee House Gallery, telling the history and showing the impact upon the town and the surrounds during both of the war periods and in between.

Penlee House itself was purchased by Penzance Town Council to serve as a war memorial after World War II. The Memorial Garden and Chapel with a Book of Remembrance adjoins the Museum in Morrab Road.

Bombs dropped in the Penzance area on a total of 867 occasions, though on the whole it was considered a fairly safe area where evacuees from other parts of the country and abroad were sent. Pool records that in a two year period, 1940-42, 16 people were killed and 48 houses totally destroyed. Some 3,750 homes in the area sustained some form of damage."Throughout the War the Bathing Pool (the outdoor salt-water pool) and the road past it were wired off and used for an anti-aircraft battery served by the Army and by the local Home Guard, an event of great historical interest in that the area so used included the site of the old Battery, built two centuries before for the defence of Penzance from enemies from the sea."

The poet, John Betjeman, a lover of Cornwall, had some depressing things to say about Penzance in his *Shell Guide, Cornwall*, in 1964:
"...Since the war Penzance has done much to destroy its settled and attractive character. The older houses in the narrow centre round the Market Hall have been pulled down and third-rate commercial 'contemporary' of which the Pearl Assurance Building is a nasty example,

are turning it into a Slough. Behind "the Abbey" on Abbey Slip are good examples of modern development by private people which could show the corporation how to fill in the gaps it has made in the old parts of the town by.slum clearance."

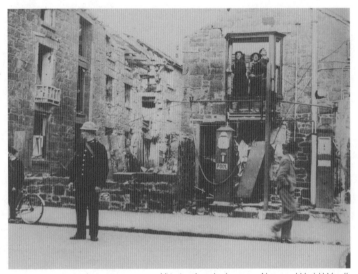

Viewing bomb damage, Alverton, World War II

One would like to be able to write that by 2000 there seems to be a turn-around in the field of town-planning and civic architecture. Perhaps there is some improvement, and certainly a positive sign has been the construction of a modern and well-kept shopping 'mall', The Wharfside, opening to the largest municipal car park at the sea-front. But, the days of small, independent shops that gave Penzance its very special character, are indeed gone for the present with few exceptions. The multiples have moved in, along with out-of-town supermarkets, and all of this collaborates in making Market Jew Street something of a clone of high streets anywhere. Small and friendly trade was always the hallmark of the market town of Penzance, and still is. The promise is there, with the idea of farmers' markets returning.

Fishing for change as well
Not much to do with fishing, but lots to do with living, housing development at Newlyn caused havoc and near riot again in 1936. A large group of houses, mostly belonging to fishermen and situated on the harbour front, were considered by the Penzance Corporation to be unfit for habitation. With the best of intentions, the suggestion was that the cottages be pulled down, and the fishermen re-housed on the Gwavas housing estate going up at the top of Chywoone Hill. Anguish and fury, 'great resentment and misunderstanding' (P. Pool) ensued. To further their protest, nine Newlyn fishermen, carrying the cheer and support of hundreds of supporters who rallied to see them away, sailed the fishing vessel Rosebud to London's Westminster Pier. Met by their M.P. and taken to the Ministry of Health, they carried a petition of over a thousand signatures protesting against the compulsory purchase of their property and the "wholesale destruction of their village". A compromise was reached, some re-building accomplished with skill, and some cottages remain.

Frank Ruhrmund in 1995 had something to say about this:
"Looking at Newlyn today it is, perhaps, difficult to appreciate the delight artists once found in the village. There have been so many changes that the Newlyn of 1995 is a far cry from "the cluster of grey-roofed houses" which Forbes found it to be in 1884 when he first "came along that dusty road by which Newlyn is approached from Penzance". Since then, and particularly in the late 1930's, it has been so plundered and abused by authority, by developers and so-called planners, that little of its former glory remains. Yet, if one looks closely enough -- digs deeply enough -- one might even excavate an actual Newlyner, and find sufficient forgotten corners to remind one of the attractiveness that was Newlyn's."

'Hear hear'! The galleries, the ship chandlers, the Fish Festival, aside from the docks themselves and the fish offer much that should not be missed. Stretching up the hill and away from the docks are large open garden areas containing the often timber-built studios used by the early artists of the Newlyn school. Even that excellent magazine of current events, *Inside Cornwall*, is published from the Fradgen in Newlyn, not a shout away from the fishermen at the piers. Certainly it can be said to be 'inside Cornwall'.

The Royal National Lifeboat Institution (RNLI)
Penzance had the distinction of being the first Cornish port to have a
lifeboat. By public subscription, she was provided for service in 1803, but
not required for rescue, so never launched. In 1824, the seedlin
organisation "to preserve life from shipwreck" which was to become the
RNLI, was funded voluntarily and has remained so, with only a little help
from time to time from governmental sources. Every penny of the money
raised today to fund the lifeboat is a voluntary contribution. In 1913, the
move of the station was effected from the western end of the Penzance
Promenade to the present Penlee Station on the coast road between
Newlyn and Mousehole.

Following the loss of the *Solomon Browne* from the Penlee Station in
December of 1981, the tragic accident that visibly touched the nation,
another voluntary crew had come forward within the hour. In 1983 the
Mabel Alice was launched as named by HRH The Duke of Kent, and this
remains the lifeboat for Mount's Bay to the present day.

From *The Cornishman*, 3 August, 1995
Around the coast-line of the West Country, from Mudeford to Weston-super-Mare, there
are 29 RNLI lifeboat stations, involving 17 all-weather boats capable of 18 knots, and 20
smaller, inshore boats with speeds up to 29 knots.
They are manned by volunteer crews though with the all-weather boats there is one full-
time paid crew member, usually the mechanic.
Working a "watch-on, watch-off" system, each duty crew member carries a 'bleeper' so that
for every lifeboat there is a full crew available for call, by HM Coastguard for 24 hours a day
throughout the year. There are now more than 100 women helping to crew lifeboats around
the UK.

Another Armada
In 1995, Newlyn's fisherpeople voiced fears of a Spanish invasion-- of a
slightly different sort. This was nothing to do with the 'Yorkies' from
Lowestoft, who were landing fish on a Sunday. Instead, it was the Spanish
again -- threatening to invade the 'Irish Box' (a specific area of sea
between Ireland and Cornwall, traditionally fished by the Cornish) in the

following year. And, even the Canadians from Newfoundland came to help with the protest, because they, too, were suffering from the massive Spanish fishing fleets.

The Canadian flags flew high at Newlyn, and the Spanish friends of our children, here on educational exchange, did not want to go down to the harbour area -- even for the Fish Festival. There was no violence, but tempers were frayed, and the newspapers and media were full of angry fishermen pleading their case. Who is to blame: our government, theirs, or the British fishermen who have sold their quotas? There are several stories to tell...and only with more hindsight than a very few years can a full record be made. At the 2000 Fish Festival, the Canadian fisheries minister has once again been invited to attend, and accepted. A special relationship now exists between our maritime cultures.

Elizabeth Stevenson, a director of the family firm of W Stevenson & Co, and herself a member of the Sea Fish Industry Authority for the UK, announced her reasons for disquiet in 1995:
"The Cornish fishing industry wants the Government to withdraw from the European Common Fisheries Policy (CFP), and reinforce a 200-mile limit around the British coast...The CFP has done nothing but slowly destroy the Cornish industry over the past two decades...The danger is from the Spanish, fishing with under-sized nets and catching under-sized species, which are the breeding stock..."

Nick Howell and his French wife, Marie Therese, opened, also in 1995, one of the most instructive and interesting standing exhibitions available in the area. At Tolcarne, in the Newlyn Coombe, visitors to the fisheries, will find 'The Pilchard Works'.

From *The Cornishman*, 3 August, 1995
"Here visitors can see for themselves not only the pressing and packing of the fish, but also a remarkable exhibition on Newlyn's history, with its work-day and social life. In the many rooms, and on various levels of this 1874 granite building, a human picture unfolds of the

fisherman, the fishing port, its characters and its many facets of interest...
" ...Records of the Cornish catches are rare prior to the 16th C. But exports of salted pilchards from Cornwall are clearly recorded in 1555, and the industry was well established by the late 1790s with exports to Italy, France and Spain...in 1905 Signor Enrico Borzone arrived in Cornwall from Genoa to buy the pressed salt pilchards...from Martin Hunkin and the business grew until in 1931 Enrico's son took over in Italy at the same time as Pawlyn Bros bought Mr. Hunkin's business...The two families carried on working together for 35 years until Shippams purchased the Newlyn business. In Italy the son of the next generation of the Borzone family took over from his father...In 1981 Mr. Howell bought the factory from Shippams and continues to trade with Giorgio Borzone..." The greatest catch was in the season of 1871 at St. Ives, when 43,500 hogsheads were exported from Cornwall. With 3,000 pilchards in a hogshead," said Nick, "a total of over 130 million fish were 'tucked' in one day."

The Fish Festival

Each summer since 1991, the Royal National Mission to Deep Sea Fishermen, has sponsored a bigger and better Fish Festival. Originally the 'brainy idea' (fish is good for the brain!) of Len Scott, every year has brought something different and interesting. The Charity itself is one of service and care for fishermen and their families, and it first opened in its present buildings in 1911. The Fish Festival is sponsored by them to earn much needed funds for carrying on their work of Christian mission and philanthropy -- helping by doing. By promoting the Port of Newlyn, by promoting fish as a food product, they also promote their own work.

At the Festival fishing displays of all kinds -- how to choose, fillet, and cook -- are added to by displays of all manner of local craft from basket-making to silver, pewter and gold jewellery, and complemented with the songs of Cornwall from the Male Choirs and local school bands. The Newlyn Art Gallery also joins in with special displays and 'tea treats'. It is the ideal opportunity to choose your seven varieties of fish for 'Starry Gazy Pie' and something more of a challenge to create it...but possible. I have!

Lighting the way

Mousehole and Newlyn, followed now by a number of other smaller villages around the Mount's Bay, put on spectacular displays of creative lighting each Advent and Christmas season. Each year fundraising and preparation precedes the wonderful night when the turning on of the lights in both harbours set the skies ablaze with lights. Another good time for a party.

The 23rd of December in Mousehole is set aside for special processions of music-makers and fancy dress, in honour of the memorable hero, Tom Bawcock. The anniversary is of the time when he managed to save the village of Mousehole, starving through lack of a catch in the terrible storms, by landing a huge shoal of fish -- enough to make the Starry Gazy Pie for the whole of the population. This story is beautifully told through the eyes of a cat in the now-famous children's book, *The Mousehole Cat.*

Farming in Madron: changing fortunes
Neighbours in our rural hamlet illustrate in summary the way that agricultural activity has gone in the past century. Of two large farming families, one couple remain. Maria and John grew up in nearby villages of Madron and Gulval.

Maria's mother's family leased a large acreage, farming corn and potatoes, sileage, keeping cattle, and doing a fair bit of cattle dealing. Cattle dealing involved all of the chores to do with animal husbandry, calfing, feeding, driving the cattle on foot to market in Penzance. They also maintained a 'killing shop', and performed these services to others around the local farms for a charge. Wool dealing was a sideline. This meant travelling around the district buying wool (sheepskins) with a horse and cart, then packing it for transport up country. Both grandparents, man and wife, worked the farm and raised five sons and two daughters.

Maria's grandfather was badly crippled in a farming accident when relatively young, and was cared for at home by the family for as long as he lived. When he died, his wife took over the farm and all of the business interests. Maria's grandmother was a strong and hard-working business-woman, with a major skill in dress-making. Not only did she continue all the businesses that she and her husband had begun, but she succeeded in purchasing two nearby farms, one with a mill. Of her seven children, one emigrated to farm in Australia, one was apprenticed to the grocery trade, another worked the mill, one girl stayed at home to help her with the business, and the others moved elsewhere to continue small farming. Most have now died, but descendants no longer farm.

Maria's paternal grandfather had worked in a Cornish mine as a hard-rock miner but lost his work when the local mine closed. So he went gold-mining in Colorado, but fairly soon came back when he didn't find his fortune. With no work prospects in Cornwall he left for Wales to work as a stone mason. There he married a Welsh wife, and with her had a son (Maria's father) who was to return to Cornwall in 1900, as a baby. In Cornwall, her grandfather worked as a mason, and her grandmother, just like her maternal grandmother, was a skilled dressmaker. Maria's father lied about his age at 15 years to join up as a dispatch rider during World War I, working on Salisbury Plain in Wiltshire. He learned to repair motors, cars and vans in the services. Returning to Cornwall, he apprenticed himself to mechanical engineering and worked at Holman's, Camborne. In World War II, he was a fire-watcher at the Penzance docks. Maria, his only child, married John, also from a farming family.

John's grandparents had six boys, the eldest of which was John's father. Because there was no mining work at the time, his grandfather went mining in South Africa. John's father being the eldest stayed behind to help his mother look after the family on their Penwith farm. Two of John's uncles emigrated to work in the car factories in Detroit, first one went then wrote home for his brother. Returning later to Cornwall, one became a blaster (explosives) at the Geevor Mine. Another uncle farmed, another became a blacksmith, and the youngest was a part-time market gardener, part-time farmer. John's father went on working the family farm until he died. He encouraged his son to take up an industrial trade, so John, too, became a mechanical engineer and worked at Holman's.

Maria and John met because they attended the same village schools, and from the time they walked out together in the late 1950s, their Sunday ritual was the same. Church-going at the Church of England in the village in the morning, home for lunch in their respective villages. Then together with other young people they would walk the two to three miles into Penzance to gather at the Promenade. There was a bandstand, and music provided by the Salvation Army and sometimes the Silver Band. They would then walk back in groups of two, three or more to their villages, to be home by 9pm at the latest. After they were married in 1961, they stopped attending the Prom. But, they are not alone in bemoaning the passing of this weekly event. Growing up in the Penzance area included the Promenade.

They know virtually everything there is to know about the families of Penwith, farmers and others. None of their family had ever been in fishing, but they have done most everything else there was to do, part-time and full-time. Though Maria's mother was a farmer, and father an engineer, Maria became a skilled administrator and worked for local government. Maria and John have no children.

'Keepers of our past': museums, galleries, libraries
The 20th C. in Penzance, as in many other places far and wide, has meant change at an accelerated pace. The terrible upheaval of two World Wars and the loss of so many young sons, brothers and fathers changed the social order forever. Old trades passed away as new technologies, many of them speeded on by the urgency of war needs, built up through research, one upon another from discoveries and inventions in the previous century. None of this was unique to Penzance or Cornwall.

The steam engine, the beam engine, the telephone, electricity, the motor car, the tractor, the airplane, the radio, the television, the computer, the digital age -- all means of getting something or someone from here to there quicker. Documenting how Penzance and the outlying areas of West Cornwall made its own changes in response to the 'big picture' of technological change, is the job of historians, oral and written and the job of the 'keepers' of our past. Thankfully we have a healthy and inspired batch of helpers in this enterprise, enough to keep a range of cultural organisations alive and growing. Though this book is not intended as a guidebook, rather an aid to the readers' memory of the place and its history, it is important to know how our memories are kept and restored.

Penlee House Gallery and Museum, situated in its own lovely gardens, is a prime example of a town project 'to remember and appreciate our past', taken on initially as a War Memorial in 1946 by the Borough Council of Penzance. Originally a large home constructed for the Branwell family in 1861, on a 15 acre site in Morrab Road, its use as a public building is ideal, with the libraries, Art School and St. John's Hall nearby. Its amenities include an Open Air Theatre, where repertory groups can stage productions in summer. Tennis courts, a play school, and parking accommodation completes an excellent cultural campus in the centre of the town.

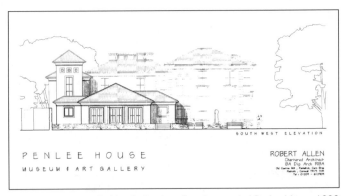

Architect's drawing of newly-extended Penlee House, 1998

Building upon a nucleus of collections made by the Penzance Natural History and Antiquarian Society (1839 -1961), and the skills of innovative curators, Penlee House has become an educational and lively social centre. Of special interest are its collection of paintings by the Newlyn School of painters, and displays of the arts and crafts related to businesses and industries of the area: such as Newlyn copper, and Crysede textiles. Its yearly programme includes permanent displays, lectures, exhibitions, and publications in association with other organisations. Renovations in the last three years of the century has ensured improved exhibition halls, a modern cafè with outdoor facility called 'The Orangery' and museum shop.

Morrab Library
No more special place exists for people with the 'reading bug' than the ever so slightly hidden treasure of the Morrab Library, situated in the Morrab Gardens near the old town bandstand. Starting out life in Penzance in that golden age of societies, the first quarter of the 19th C., it first shared premises with the Geological Society in North Parade. Both of these Societies, the Library and the Geological Society, moved to the new public buildings (St. John's Hall) in 1867. The Library then moved on, but still as a tenant of the Penzance Borough, to Morrab House, in the public gardens that the Borough purchased in 1866.

One of the few remaining private-subscription (membership organisation), circulating libraries in Britain, the Morrab is a thriving community of local historians and readers of all ages. Its new scheme of scholarships, given by internationally famous author John le Carre, who also serves as its inspiring President, offers pupils and students their own carrel and a stipend to employ its facilities to their potential.

Today in 2000, the Royal Geological Society Museum, with its wonderful geological displays, remains in the newly-renovated west wing of St. John's Hall and welcomes visitors. It focuses on the geology of the planet with special emphasis on Cornwall's importance in the field of mineralogy. If science and communications is the tourist's bent, both the Goonhilly Earth Station on the Lizard, and the Museum at the former Cable and Wireless College at Porthcurno can be visited, illustrating the premier position that West Cornwall has held in transatlantic communications history. An

outstanding heritage centre for those interested in mining history is to be found at Geevor Tin Mine, Pendeen, where visitors can see a steam operated beam engine at work.

On with the show!
Any history of the arts and crafts of the Penzance area must include mention of the thriving theatrical and musical groups that contribute so much to the life of the area. Today we have the newly refurbished Acorn Theatre as an excellent venue for both professional and amateur events. The auditorium of St. John's Hall also plays host to larger and usually operatic productions, whereas the world famous Minack outdoor theatre at nearby Porthcurno, cut into the cliffs, draws theatre companies from everywhere.

The 19th C. tradition of Church choirs and bands has helped the Penzance area in the 20th C to develop an enviable reputation for musical excellence. In 1975 the Marazion Apollo Male Voice Choir, founded in 1904, came second to a Bulgarian state choir in the male voice section of the famous Llangollen International Eisteddfod, and in 1987 first in a select gathering of premier national male choirs at Nelson. It has the distinction of being the first male choir in Cornwall. John J. Matthews, who conducted at Llangollen, achieved second place with the Penzance Ladies Orpheus at the Third Malta International Festival in 1991.

Touring has become a marked feature of musical life. The Penzance Youth Wind Band under Paul Carter visited San Francisco and Grass Valley in 1998, as part of an exchange with Cornish communities in California. They were followed to west-coast America by the Mousehole Male Voice Choir, under the baton of Tommy Waters, in 1999. At the same time, Newlyn Male Choir, led by John Phillpotts, were singing in Westminster Abbey, London, following an invitation from the Abbey's Newlyn-born deputy organist, John Hosking. This was combined with a concert at Windsor, where the guest soloist was Richard Jackson, Professor of German Song at the Royal Academy of Music. Although Jackson now has an international reputation, his debut was as a nervous Penzance teenager on the stage of St. John's Hall.

For many people February each year is lightened by productions of the Penzance Amateur Operatic Society. Starting in the season 1926-7, the society has developed an extensive repertoire, including, of course, *The Pirates of Penzance*. Its performance in 1993, of *The Gondoliers* by Gilbert and Sullivan, under the stage direction of Alistair Donkin, formerly of the D'Oyle Carte, and musical direction of the late Bernard Williams, won the prestigious Award for Regional Excellence given by the National Operatic and Dramatic Association.

Penzance has the rare distinction of possessing its own choral society, for many years the province of Dr. Edward Weymouth, and symphony orchestra. The more intimate Sinfonia of St. Mary's, conducted by Russell Jory and led by Joyce Preston, has done much to stimulate the town's young amateur and professional talent. An early music group, the Belerion Consort, performs under the inspiration of Anthony White, who also specialises in making his own period instruments. The lovely soprano voice of Catherine Pearce is frequently heard at their concerts.

A much rejuvenated town band is now gaining itself a reputation at contest and concert and is doing much for young players in the area. The Peninsula choir, the Richmond Ladies, and the Govenek, a popular religious choir formed through the vision of its young conductor Stephen Lawry, gives an idea of the range of music available. Few places can have a higher percentage of its population involved in playing and performing.

Essential to the local theatrical scene have been a host of hard-working playwrights, actors and repertory groups. They live a notoriously precarious existence, as all players wander far and wide looking for work and opportunity to strut their stuff. The Acorn Theatre as a venue, and the Arts Club nearby help to support the 'poor artists' of the stage and screen who make Penzance and area their home. Promotion is all important and in this line, Martyn Val Baker, a printer, a Gallery owner, and not least an organiser of local events and festivals in both Penzance and St. Ives, serves more than most. Selfless and hard-working, he like his father before him, Denys Val Baker (publisher and author) does much to document the arts scene.

A professional acting troupe called Theatre Rotto, headed by actor and playwright, Julia McLean, busily lead a national, international and local schedule of performances -- musical and theatrical. Aside from local work-shops and performances for schools, Theatre Rotto initiated several puppet festivals in the 1990s culminating in a very successful International Puppet Festival with troupes from Eastern Europe, Switzerland, Africa and the USA participating. In 1999, they were winners at the International Celtic Film Festival for their animated puppet film made jointly with Alison de Vere Animation, and Three SSS Films, taken from a local legend, *How Madge Figgey got her Pig*. One of a projected series, entitled *Tales from the Land's End*, these cooperating creators are keeping the old tradition of Cornish droll-telling alive in a contemporary medium.

Local playwright, Pauline Sheppard, had great success with her play, *Dressing Granite*, and continues to write plays alongside her post as Arts Coordinator of Penwith District Council. Together with David Shaw, Pauline was a prime mover in the late Shiva Theatre, which later was to become the Penzance-based Cornwall Theatre Company, making the Acorn Theatre its home.

It is impossible to mention all the groups, large and small, who increase the colour and entertainment value of our cultural lives, but that is not to say they are not noticed or listened to with eagerness. The celebrations of Golowan, the annual festival of the midsummer Feast of St. John, emphasizes this fact.

Transport and Media today
The march of the media in the 20th C. has been equalled by the race of

the writers, journalists and designers to find themselves a quiet corner where they can create. Though the distance has not changed between Land's End and London, and even though almost all else has, there are now several ways to approach. Automobile is undoubtedly the firm favourite, as tailbacks on summer weekends will show. But there are other possibilities and foreign tourists are most likely to arrive on the railway as they have throughout the century. The railway station is the original one designed to provide a smaller version of Paddington Station in London 'at the other end'. It sits on the eastern side of the town centre, conveniently located at the bottom of Market Jew Street. Taxis are aplenty and service the whole district of West Cornwall. A new Visitor Centre, with tourist guidebooks and lists of local accommodation, is located between the train station and the bus terminus, both located side by side within metres of the sea front.

Tourist and charter air services have been available since 1964 from the Penzance heliport at Eastern Green and from the Lands End Airport. The latter links with Newquay, Plymouth, Exeter and Bristol, and also provides flight tuition for beginners and the more experienced. Both of these air services, together with *Scillonian III* and the *Gry Maritha* by sea, offer passenger and freight passage to the Isles of Scilly.

At the last census (1991), Penzance remained the largest town in Penwith, with a population of approximately 13,000 with another 7,000 in the surrounding area. St. Ives with 7,039 and Hayle with 7,335 come joint second within the district council area, and St. Just, the most westerly, with 4,475 people. The largest employers in the area are those of health services, education, and government agencies, and as a group the hoteliers and catering establishments. Though the most important port in the country by value of fish landed, the fishing industry like that of agriculture and manufacturing are declining in relation to jobs available. Characterised now by seasonal and fairly low-paid work, west Cornwall including Hayle, is an area of high unemployment, at least 2% higher than the rest of the county.

Since the 1870s, *The Cornishman* newspaper, now part of a group linked to the Western Morning News (Plymouth) that provides a daily paper for the whole of the region, has served as the major 'local' weekly for Penzance and area. BBC Radio Cornwall maintains a local link station and dedicated reporter to the primary station in Truro, and a number of other independent stations are operational in the county. Both BBC Television and West Country/Carleton (ITV) cover Cornish news from their separate bases in Plymouth.

Friends in deed
The 20th C. has brought not only world wars and latterly Balkan and European unrest, but also reconciliation and the furthering of twinning arrangements between towns and cities on the continent and in Britain. The German port town of Cuxhaven is one partner of Penzance (taken over by the Penwith District Council in 1974), and another is, most appropriately, Concarneau in Brittany (1981). Latterly (1998) a further twinning partnership has been entered with the City of Bendigo in Australia. Exchanges and events take place intermittently and when each town can fit special visits to each other, in their own busy schedules of civic activities. As detailed in the sections on fishing, many friendly ties have also been forged between the Canadian coastal states of Nova Scotia (New Scotland) and Newfoundland with our port of Newlyn.

The Festival Year
Little information has been threaded through this book about the feast days, festivals and folk customs that attend each year of the town of Penzance and the villages around the Mount's Bay. This has been deliberate because of the complex nature and diversity of the celebrations, and their various and separate histories.

There are numerous studies of the common tradition in the folklore of Western Europe, but always there are local variations, influenced by geography, religion, local heroes and all the other topics raised in this book. Though less in the western half of Cornwall than in the eastern, the modes and methods of celebration have inevitably been influenced by English ways. Some of the traditions handed down to us are vague and quite general at best, leaving open the interpretation of what is meant. The mixture of language with legend, without an accompanying early written literature, is also something of a shroud to any full understanding of what actually happened in the far distant past. Nevertheless, these facts set us free to celebrate our heritage in new ways, built upon the customs of past people but creating new traditions of our own.

Even within the small geographical area of Penwith, there are different and specific customs, superstitions, and traditional celebrations. Each of the villages has their separate feast day, based on their patron saint, but undoubtedly as explained in Chapter 1, taken over in spirit and somewhat in practice from ancient Celtic festivals of the two seasons: Beltane, the first of May eve, being the beginning of summer, and Samhain, the first of November eve, being the beginning of winter. The ancient Celtic year began with Samhain, and was marked by three quarter days which followed, Imbolc (the eve of the first of February), Beltane, and Lughnasadh (the eve of the first of August). Each was the occasion for a festival, and parts of these celebration customs continue today.

Penzance has taken up the remembrance of its Celtic and Cornish past in a unique way that knits the community together, and it seems to grow bigger and better each year. The Golowan Festival is based around the celebration of the midsummer Feast of St. John (Gol-Jowan, Cornish language). A full fortnight of musical and theatrical events, markets and street performances unfolds, climaxing with the colourful processions and dances on Mazey Day. The ancient Quay Fair, has also been combined with Golowan, and complements the Festival with side shows, Edwardian-style rides, pub music and free entertainments on the streets. Fireworks conclude the celebrations.

The Penzance historian, Douglas Williams, writes:
"For hundreds of years Golowan was celebrated in Penzance on Midsummer Eve, June 23,

and St. John's Day on June 24. There were processions of burning torches through the town, tar barrels rolling down the streets, fireworks, bonfires, the ancient Serpent Dance led by the bizarre 'Penglax', and the election of the Mock Mayor of the Quay...Attempts to ban these lively "dangerous entertainments" were finally successful in 1877, but in 1929 the bonfire festival on John's Eve was revived by the Old Cornwall Societies. Many [fires] are lit on the Penzance and Penwith hilltops, forming a 'chain' from Chapel Carn Brea near Land's End to Kit Hill, close to the Cornish border.
The year 2000 is the tenth anniversary of the local revival of the Feast of St. John celebrations, and Golowan director, Stephen Hall, with the support of the Town Council and many others, has emphasised the Millennium year in the most dramatic and colourful way possible."

In legend and literature

Penzance remains an important centre of literary and cultural activity. The Cornish cultural revival of the twentieth-century brought about renewed interest in many of the writers, narratives and poetry that emerged from Penzance over the centuries. This revival, coupled with the decline of industrial infrastructure in Cornwall at the end of the nineteenth-century, meant that a new cultural order or means of survival would have to be found, if Penzance itself were not to close for business.

Tourism seemed the way forward. Penzance was marketed as a Mediterranean-style holiday destination, enhanced with posters and merchandising from the Great Western Railway. The latter projected the Penzance area in particular as 'a land of legend' and sold the town on bright, attractive pictures. Progressively this has led, throughout the 19th and 20th centuries, to a mass conversion of some larger houses in the centre into B&B (Bed and Board) accommodation, the construction of further hotels, and more recently into the provision of self-catering holiday lets. Not to be held up as literature, but certainly of interest in itself, are the many tourist leaflets, advertising brochures, and tourist guides available to the public and to the visitor. Business directories, catalogues, all manner of written information are available, and now, of course, Penzance also has its websites on the Internet for the websurfer.

The various schools of artists who settled around the area allowed for a new direction for cultural development, projecting the town as an artistic and literary centre. They produced paintings that would visually excite the far-flung interest of collectors, curators, and not least, to engage the curiosity of their real-life models and their descendants. In the latter years of the 20th C. their lives and works have served to draw the interest of further generations of artists, writers, art and literary historians. The creation of the West Cornwall Art Archive in 1995, contributes to that renaissance of interest. Situated temporarily at the Jamieson Library, Newmill, this Archive and Library is currently seeking to re-locate into the central cultural zone of Penzance and will probably achieve this within the year 2000.

In their own time, the artists were teachers and lecturers as well. John D. MacKenzie and some of his fellow artists were to initiate and establish the Newlyn Copper workshops, which gave employment and new skills to fishermen who for one reason or another could not continue to fish. Some, like Stanhope Forbes lectured to learned societies such as the Morrab Library, and not least, some were also writers. Norman Garstin, in particular, wrote regularly for art magazines and journals, and his son, Crosbie Garstin, became a highly regarded Cornish genre novelist.

A good example of a writer and artist was Elizabeth Armstrong Forbes, a Canadian by birth but well-travelled and trained in art before moving to west Cornwall to join the painters at Newlyn. In 1889, she married Stanhope Forbes and ten years later they opened The Newlyn School of Painting, using their studios and the Meadow at Newlyn for indoor and outdoor studios. Articles began to appear in national magazines and journals about their training school and many pupils were to come from London and elsewhere to receive their tuition. Some of these would become professional artists in their own right, others continuing with arts and crafts in a more amateur fashion, as a sideline to their main occupations.

In 1905, Elizabeth was to write and illustrate a most spectacular book, which was devised as a gift to her son. *King Arthur's Wood* is a book with two stories in it: 'King Arthur's Wood, A Fairy Story' and told with it, 'Sir Gareth of Orkney and ye Lady of ye Castle Perilous'. A copy of this outsized book is now a collector's item, but can be seen at Penlee House. The scenes in this book are from the landscape of Land's End, and incorporate that major legend once again, of our hero Arthur. In summer, 2000, at Penlee House Gallery, Elizabeth's paintings are featured in a major travelling exhibition. For the first time she has been given a solo show of work, with a book illustrating her importance in the world of art, *Singing from the Walls, The life and work of Elizabeth Armstrong Forbes*.

Perhaps the most established poet of the area in the post-war period has been Frank Ruhrmund. His knowledge of the fishing communities around Penzance, Newlyn and Mousehole is second-to-none; his poetry encapsulates much of the ideology and landscape of the west Cornwall area. 'Night' from his 1976 collection *Penwith Poems* seems to captures this:

> The dark-bound harbour is quiet,
> deaf to the tar-bound traffic
> that growls streaming by it.
>
> A late boat with green lights and red
> glides in its wave-hungry mouth,
> Creeps cat-like purring to bed.
>
> A beery man feels his bilge-swilled way
> down one arm of rope and rings,
> careful of greasy steps that sway.
>
> Sea-wracked cottages wallow in dream
> of new-nailed wood and fresh paint,
> lullabied at berth by lighthouse beams.

As well as writers such as Ruhrmund there has been the extraordinary success of the children's book *The Mousehole Cat* (1990) by Antonia Barber and Nicola Bayley. Theirs is a re-telling of the story of Tom Bawcock -- and how he saved Mousehole from famine, a legend mentioned earlier which brings with it a yearly celebration on the 22nd of December.

In the 20th C. in the Land's End area, we have a cultural and literary plenty, perhaps a harvest of plenty. There are novelists, playwrights, poets, art historians, local history buffs, as well as literary and artistic organisations by the dozen. To mention only one or two as has been done, is something of a travesty. But lack of space is the plea. There is no sign that this revival of interest in legends and in practicalities of survival is on the wane. Numerous people are contributing to the panorama in their separate ways, and plenty of quite ordinary but exceedingly creative people have positive ideas for our future. We do look to our past both as a source and a resource. But, we have our eyes turned forward.

These warriors and dear women, whom
I've called, as bidden, from the tomb,
May not have failed to raise
An antique spell at moments here?
--They were, in their long-faded sphere,
As you are now who muse thereat;
Their mirth, crimes, fear and love begat
Your own, though thwart their ways;
And may some pleasant thoughts outshape
From this my conjuring to undrape
Such ghosts of distant days!

From Thomas Hardy in the guise of Merlin, Epilogue
The Famous Tragedy of the Queen of Cornwall, At Tintagel in Lyonnesse

Reading Trail for Chapter 4

Denys Val Baker (1949 -51 1st series) *The Cornish Review*, Lelant: D.V. Baker.

Antonia Barber and Nicola Bayley (1990), *The Mousehole Cat*, London: Walker.

Sheila Bird (1987) *Bygone Penzance and Newlyn*, Chichester: Phillimore.

Katherine Bradley (2000) *Women's Suffrage Movement in Cornwall*, 1870-1914, Penzance: The Hypatia Trust.

Ithell Colquhoun (1957) *The Living Stones*, London: Peter Owen.

Nick Darke (1999) *The Riot*, London: Methuen Drama.

Des Hannigan (1999) *Francis Frith's Around Penzance*, Photographic Memories, Salisbury: Frith Book Company.

Melissa Hardie (1995) *100 Years in Newlyn, Diary of a Gallery*, Patten Press in association with the Newlyn Art Gallery.

Jonathan Holmes (1992) *Penzance and Newlyn in Old Photographs*, Stroud: Alan Sutton Publishing, and (1996) *Mount's Bay*, Stroud: Alan Sutton; The Archive Photograph Series.

Jim Hosking (1999) *Boskenna & the Paynters*, Penzance: J.M. Hosking.

Alan Kent (1998) *'Wives, Mothers and Sisters': Feminism, Literature and Women Writers in Cornwall*, Penzance: The Hypatia Trust.

John Curnow Laity (1986) *Newlyn Copper*, Penzance Town Council.

Cyril Noall (1978) *The Illustrated Past: Penwith, An Historical Survey of the Land's End District*, Buckingham: Barracuda Books.

Frank Ruhrmund, (1974) *Penwith Poems*, Padstow: Lodenek Press.

Douglas Williams (1993) *About Penzance*

Index of people, places & themes

Dawns Myin,
Boleigh, Parish of St Buryan, Cornwall.
Published by Henry Besley, Exeter.